MEDIUMS
AND THE

Linda Williamson is a
tary of the Wimbledon
London. A freelance cc
Worlds and other public
in Spiritualism for a n........ .. j.... .. ..
and lecturer, and has made an extensive study of the
subject of mediumship. She is married and lives in
Wimbledon. Her first book, *Mediums and their Work*,
was also published by Robert Hale.

By the same author

Mediums and their Work

LINDA WILLIAMSON

Mediums
and the Afterlife

ROBERT HALE · LONDON

ISBN 0 7090 5414 9

Robert Hale Limited
Clerkenwell House
Clerkenwell Green
London EC1R 0HT

Photoset in North Wales by
Derek Doyle & Associates, Mold, Clwyd.
Printed in Great Britain by
St Edmundsbury Press Limited, Bury St Edmunds, Suffolk.
Bound by WBC Bookbinders Limited, Bridgend, Glamorgan.

Contents

Illustrations

Between pages 104 and 105

1 Linda Williamson
2 Psychic drawing by Rita Taylor and (inset) photograph of the same man in life
3 A materialized figure at a Helen Duncan séance
4 Jack Webber, showing the removal of his coat
5 Minnie Harrison. The ectoplasm is being used to manipulate a trumpet
6 The ghost on the television screen
7 Stephen Turoff working on a patient
8 The ghostly motor-cyclist photographed by Reg Wickens

Acknowledgements

I would like to thank all the mediums and others who gave me help and encouragement in the preparation of this book. Special thanks go to Gilbert Bonner, Tina Laurent, Stephen Turoff, Philip Steff, Stephen O'Brien and Derek Robinson, and to Tony Ortzen and Tim Haigh of *Psychic News*.

Introduction

'Do you believe in life after death?' asked the earnest young man who called at my door. I glanced down at his smart leather brief-case from which protruded a copy of *The Watchtower*. 'I should hope so,' I told him. 'I'm a medium.' The result was predictable. His jaw dropped, he snapped the brief-case shut then, without a word, he made off down the path at a great rate, slamming the gate behind him. I never saw him again.

Announcing that you are a medium produces a variety of interesting reactions, not just in Jehovah's Witnesses. Some people take an instinctive step backwards, surreptitiously making the sign of the cross. Many are politely sceptical but many others are fascinated and want to know more.

The response to my last book, *Mediums and Their Work*, was very encouraging. I was interviewed on radio stations all over the country and received dozens of letters from readers telling me about their psychic experiences. In this present book I have concentrated on aspects of mediumship which I touched on briefly before but did not have the space to explore at depth.

Ghosts, for instance; lots of people claim to see them, but what exactly are they? Are they earthbound spirits returning to haunt the places where they lived or is there another explanation? And séances; many people wanted to know if I conduct séances.

I have lost count of the number of times I have had to explain that the traditional dark séance room, with spirit forms and luminous trumpets flying around, belongs to the Victorian age rather than to the present day. Nevertheless, this form of mediumship has not completely died out. In fact, there are signs

11

that it is now enjoying a revival. So what really happens when the lights go out?

Spiritual healing is another subject which I found aroused great interest, as more and more people, alarmed at the side-effects of modern drugs are turning to holistic methods of treatment. Healing is just one such method, but modern research has proved that it can be highly successful and the medical profession is at last beginning to take it seriously.

But my main purpose in writing this book has been to look at the deepest and most fundamental mystery of all; what happens when we die, and what is the next world like? I do not claim to have all the answers; there is much that we cannot know. But there is one thing we can be sure of – that death need hold no fear; that it is the beginning of a great adventure.

1 'I Want to Come to You, Dear'

'How did you become a medium?' In the radio interviews and phone-ins that followed the publication of my book, I found that question cropping up again and again.

To me, my ability has always been something natural. As a child, long before I was introduced to Spiritualism or even knew what a medium was, I used to sense the presence of spirit people around me and hear voices in my head. This didn't frighten me. I accepted it, as children do accept these things, as a normal part of life. But at the same time, something warned me that, if I spoke about it, I would be regarded as odd, if not mad, so for years I kept my experiences to myself. It was part of my inner, secret world, along with the stories I wove in my head and the make-believe characters with which, as an only child, I shared my solitude.

As I grew older I decided that the voices were probably make-believe as well – until they started telling me about things that were going to happen. The predictions were only of trivial events, but when they came true I was shocked. I began to question my own sanity and didn't know where to turn for help.

It was a book that came to my rescue – *Where Two Worlds Meet*, by the Spiritualist writer Arthur Findlay, in which he describes a series of sittings he had with the medium John Sloane. Now that I realized that my voices were speaking to me from the world beyond, I wanted to know more about this gift I was privileged to possess. I read every book I could find on the subject and started attending Spiritualist churches. It was at the church in Wimbledon, to which I still belong, that I was invited to join what is called a development circle, a group in which mediums are trained.

I went along to the first meeting with great anticipation. I had imagined that it was something like the Magic Circle. I believed

13

that once you were admitted to such a group you were let into the mysterious secrets of how to do it, and suddenly you were able to see and hear the spirit people as clearly as you could see and hear people in this life.

To my disappointment, nothing of the sort happened. I discovered that there are no mysterious secrets. Developing mediumship is a gradual process of making the mind more sensitive and more receptive to the world of spirit. There are no short cuts – it just takes regular meditation and practice. And even when you've been doing it for years, it's never easy.

'Do you see spirits all the time?' one interviewer wanted to know, adding, with a nervous glance around the studio, 'Can you see anyone here now?'

'No,' I replied quite truthfully. 'Unless I'm actually working psychically I "switch off" so that the spirit world doesn't intrude into my everyday life. If I wasn't able to do that, I'd probably be a nervous wreck by now!'

In fact, mediums don't 'see' as much as people think they do. Very few of them see spirits in the same clear, solid way we see people on this plane. Some mediums can do this but for most, like myself, it's a different sort of perception, hard to describe, something between seeing and sensing. Similarly, the voices I hear are like the ones I heard as a child, not external but inside my head. At the same time, I get mental pictures and 'feel' the characters of those communicating, and all these senses are used in combination. I can only speak for myself however. Every medium works in a slightly different way. Some never see or hear anything, but work by sensation alone.

'Can anyone do it?' was another frequent question. If a person has the potential for mediumship, it usually shows itself at an early age. Nevertheless, I always advise anyone who is seriously interested to join a church and get themselves into a circle. You never know what you can do until you try! I know of mediums who claim that they had never had a psychic experience in their lives, yet, as soon as they started sitting in a circle, their gift suddenly started to unfold, much to their own surprise. On the other hand, some people never develop any ability, no matter how hard they try. In theory, it should be possible for anyone to do it. We are all spirits here and now, even while we are encased in physical bodies, so we should be able to commune with spirits without bodies. But a person's potential may be too deeply buried to be brought to the surface – the material mind which says 'I can't' gets in the way and the spirit communicators simply can't get through.

'Isn't it wrong to call up the dead?' This anxiety has been expressed to me many times. It's one of the most common misapprehensions about Spiritualism and always has mediums jumping up and down with indignation. The fact is that we do not call up the dead – they call us up. No one can be forced to come back if they don't want to. Mediums simply provide a channel for those who do wish to make contact with their loved ones on earth.

The word 'dead' is one I don't like using. There is no such thing as death. To die is simply to shed the physical body and enter into the spirit world. However, I equally dislike euphemisms such as 'passed on', 'passed over' or 'been promoted'. I'm not even sure I like the habit mediums have of referring to people as being 'in spirit'. A former editor of the *Psychic News*, Maurice Barbanell, forbade the use of the expression in his paper, saying that it sounded as though they had been pickled! So I will say 'dead' when I mean 'dead' – but my definition is 'still living, but in a higher dimension'.

Having optimistically written in my first book that the image of the medium is changing and that the public as a whole has a clearer conception of what mediums are and what they do, I was disappointed to discover from the comments I received how deeply engrained the traditional image of the Madame Arcati medium and the eerie séance room is. You know the sort of thing I mean; the circle of people holding hands round the table in a dark room.

'Is there anybody there? One rap for no, two for yes.'

The table raps twice.

'Is that you, Aunty Ada?' Rap, rap.

'Have you got a message for anyone here?'

Thump, thump, goes the table leg.

The medium, a plump little old lady sitting at the end of the table, begins to breathe heavily then her eyes roll and she falls into a trance.

'Talk to us, Aunt Ada!'

'Hello!' The medium's voice is laboured. 'It's me, Ada.'

'What's it like where you are, Aunty?' someone asks, and the sitters wait with bated breath for the revelations from the other side.

'It's lovely here, Uncle George is with me. I'm so happy.'
And so on.

It really isn't like that at all. Speaking personally, I have never
sat in a dark room holding hands round a table. I doubt whether
I could produce ectoplasm if I tried and, as for trance, I'm afraid
I never could quite get the hang of it. Like most mediums today,
I work in the light and in a normal state of consciousness,
either taking services in Spiritualist churches or giving private
sittings.

Many people don't realize that Spiritualist churches exist.
There are in fact hundreds of them, in this country and abroad.
Spiritualism is a recognized religion. My own church is one of
the biggest and the most well-known and attracts many
newcomers.

I am aware that the word 'spiritualism' puts many people off.
Some of those who come to our church for the first time,
brought in reluctantly by friends who have been there before,
can be seen looking around nervously wondering when the
ghosts are going to appear. They are pleasantly surprised to find
a simple service basically like that of any other church. There is
a conspicuous absence of dogma and preaching. One young
man who joined us recently confided to me that he was relieved
that no one had tried to save his soul!

Each service contains a short demonstration of mediumship,
called clairvoyance, when the medium will attune to the spirit
world and pass on short 'messages' to members of the
congregation. These messages come in for a lot of ridicule. It
has been commented disparagingly that they contain nothing
but trivia and that, if the dead haven't got something more
important to say, they might as well not bother coming back.

I can understand this criticism. Messages like 'Uncle Fred's
bringing you a beautiful bunch of violets' and 'Aunt Flo says, do
you remember the trouble she used to have with her false teeth?'
don't do much to encourage the serious investigator intent on
discovering the ultimate purpose of existence.

Mediums themselves don't always do much for the
Movement's image.

'I want to come to you, dear. Have you got a father in the
world of spirit? No? A grandfather, then ... what about a
father-in-law?'

It is sad that in some ways Spiritualism has become the victim of its own success. There are so many churches, particularly in the London area, each holding at least two services a week. Mediums have to be found to take them and because there are not enough good mediums to go round, the standard has fallen over the last few years.

But on the plus side, there are some excellent mediums, sincere and dedicated people, and many of the best ones don't make the headlines. Not all messages are trivial. The names, descriptions and information given are often very accurate. Even minor details, which may be dismissed by other listeners as trivia, can be highly significant for the person for whom they are intended.

Once the mechanics of mediumship is understood, the reason for the apparently trivial nature of the messages becomes clear. Spiritualism is, for the most part, concerned with contacting those who have only recently passed into the next world. Their personalities are unchanged – we do not sprout wings when we die. If, say, your father comes back and tries to reach you through a medium, his first concern will be to prove to you that it really is him. To do this he will try to give his name, if he can, then he will talk about whatever is uppermost in his mind, perhaps recalling his last days on earth, mentioning events that are going on in your life or sending his love to other members of the family. It is rather as if he had emigrated to Australia and was giving you a ring to let you know he has arrived safely. He will not come back and launch into an erudite lecture about life, the universe and everything. For one thing he will not have been there long enough to find out and, for another, if he spoke in a way that was so out of character you would not know it was him.

Another point that is not sufficiently realized is that communication is very difficult, from both sides of life. I explained in *Mediums and Their Work* some of the problems involved. From the medium's point of view, these problems can be very frustrating. I wish I could say to a sitter, 'I have your father here. His name was Joe Bloggs and he lived at 37 Acacia Avenue and died in 1973 of a heart attack.' Unfortunately, it doesn't work like that. The impressions a medium receives are frequently hazy. They have to try to sense what is coming through and put it into words as clearly as they can.

It is no doubt equally frustrating for those trying to communicate, when they cannot even get a simple name across.

For someone in the spirit world, trying to get through at a public meeting and competing with crowds of others all wanting to speak to the medium at the same time, it must be like trying to make yourself heard in a football stadium in the middle of a match. This is why I recommend anyone who is seriously interested in investigating the subject to go for a private sitting with a good medium. It is easier for a medium to work on a one-to-one basis and in a relaxed atmosphere so the results are likely to be better.

There is nothing in Spiritualism to be afraid of. This is a point I constantly emphasize, since it is a pity that many people who could be helped in this way hold back because of fear. Whether you go for a sitting or attend a church, you will not see or hear anything spooky. I always say to anyone who is nervous, 'If things start flying around in here I'll be out of that door before you are!'

There is a popular impression that people only go to see a medium when they have been bereaved. This is, of course, the most obvious reason but it is not the only one. A lot of confusion exists as to what mediums actually do. Their function is to link the two worlds together and provide evidence of the continuity of life after physical death. They pass on whatever they receive from the spirit in the way of advice, comfort or guidance, but their concern is primarily with communication. In this they differ from psychics such as astrologers, tarot readers or palmists who focus on the person themself, their character, their life and their future.

This distinction is often not clear to sitters, who come along expecting to be told all about themselves and to have their problems solved. Some of them are actually surprised when the medium starts describing their deceased friends and relations. I've often had it said to me, 'Oh, no, it can't be him. He's dead!'

One woman came to me, very irate because her husband had run off with someone else. Would I tell her where they had gone, she demanded, because she intended to go after them and get him back. I had to inform her that locating errant husbands was not one of my skills. She departed in high dudgeon, saying that she was going to find him for herself. Whether she did, I never found out, but she was a tough lady and I wouldn't have liked to be in his shoes if she ever caught up with him!

Another woman wanted to know when her elderly mother was

going to die. I dread questions like that. I never predict death, even if I am told when a person is going to die, which I very rarely am. Poor dear, I thought, what can I say to comfort her? Her mother was ninety-five and it was obvious that she couldn't live very much longer. I needn't have worried, however. She couldn't stand her mother and what she actually wanted to know was how much longer she was going to have to put up with her!

Mediums are not fortune-tellers either. I remember one lady who asked me if she was going to win the pools.

'I'm afraid I can't tell you that,' I admitted.

'Oh.' She was clearly disappointed. 'But a medium told me in 1936 that I was going to win the pools ...'

It would have been cruel to disillusion her. 'Well, dear,' I said, 'I suggest you keep trying!'

Mediums frequently come under attack from fundamentalists who accuse them of being in league with the devil. It is not uncommon for born-again Christians to picket halls where Spiritualist meetings are being held, parading up and down outside with placards and trying to dissuade people from entering. This is very good for ticket sales. It encourages people to go in, if only to find out exactly what sort of satanic rites are being performed!

The Bible can be quoted to support any argument and there is little that can be said to those who see everyone outside their own belief system as destined irrevocably for hell. I have no sympathy with bigotry. I do, however, have much sympathy with devout and thoughtful Christians who would like to find out about life after death. They may have had psychic experiences they don't understand or may be concerned about the fate of a loved one who has died, yet feel that they cannot investigate the subject because they would be going against the dictates of their church.

I have experienced this problem for myself. When I was in my teens I attended an Anglican church, where I met many sincere and beautiful people and was in many ways very happy. But I couldn't agree with the doctrine, especially not the teachings concerning the afterlife.

Christianity has never quite made up its mind on this point. The official line is that the dead sleep in their tombs until the day of judgement, when they will be raised up in bodily form.

This is contradicted by experience and, to an extent, by the Bible itself. Jesus on the cross promised the penitent thief, 'This day thou shalt be with me in Paradise.'

When I raised this issue with the vicar, I was discouraged from asking questions and severely warned against the dangers of getting mixed up with those wicked people who call up the dead. In my innocence, I found this attitude puzzling. Surely the church taught life after death? I thought they would have been interested in evidence that backed up their teaching. But of course, I soon realized that what mediums say about the afterlife presents a very different picture from the medieval image of heaven and hell. They were a challenge to the church's authority and had to be suppressed at all costs.

My championing of their cause made me distinctly unpopular. Heretics may not be burned at the stake these days, but in some congregations they are made to feel like dangerous subversives threatening to overturn the theological apple-cart. I was so disgusted by this narrow-mindedness that I left the church altogether to pursue my search for truth elsewhere.

My own psychic experiences had drawn me towards Spiritualism and it was here that I found a belief that made sense to me. Spiritualism isn't all messages from Aunt Fanny. It has a well worked out philosophy that explains where we come from and what we are doing here, as well as telling us where we are going when we die.

Many people come into Spiritualism from the Church of England or one of the other orthodox churches and are pleased to find that they do not have to abandon the faith they are familiar with. In fact, there is a large Christian Spiritualist movement which, while not adhering rigidly to the conventional creeds, accepts Jesus Christ as its spiritual leader. Some Spiritualists disagree with this point of view. They believe that Spiritualism should stand apart from all other religions because its teachings are universal. This debate has raged almost since the beginning of the Spiritualist movement in the middle of the last century. Without going into the intricacies of the opposing arguments, suffice it to say that Spiritualism is broad enough to accommodate many different schools of thought, all of which are united by the basic tenet that life goes on after death and that communication takes place with those in the next world.

As well as withstanding attacks from orthodoxy, mediums

have to defend themselves against critics who claim that they are all frauds and charlatans who prey on the gullibility of the elderly and bereaved. It is true that there are some unscrupulous frauds about. There is nothing in law to stop anyone from setting themselves up as a medium, clairvoyant or whatever they choose to call themselves and charging exorbitant fees to those desperate enough or foolish enough to be taken in by them. The best way to avoid these rogues is to seek a personal recommendation, possibly from a church, of a reputable medium. If in doubt about the fee, ask beforehand how much they charge and if it seems too much, go elsewhere. The vast majority of mediums are honest, sincere and only charge moderate fees (some not charging at all).

Another accusation frequently made is that mediums at public meetings cheat by 'planting' accomplices in the audience then going to them with 'messages'. Again, I cannot say that this never happens. If a medium is taking a meeting in a hall or theatre with several hundred people in the audience, obviously the temptation must be there to improve their performance by ensuring that at least some of the 'messages' are accepted.

I can honestly say, however, having been backstage at many such meetings, that I have never come across any cheating. At all demonstrations of clairvoyance, as they are called, it is unnecessary to purchase tickets in advance and anyone can come in. In an average evening the medium might give fifteen or twenty messages. It is hardly feasible that all the recipients could be 'plants'. I have heard from many people who have attended such meetings and have been astonished at what the medium told them.

'Ah, yes,' the critic will allege, 'but all the medium is doing is using a little psychology, a bit of clever guesswork and rounding it off with a few platitudes of the sort that could apply to anyone.'

This is called 'cold reading', and certainly 'messages' can be made up in this way, with no help from the spirit world. For instance, it is possible to deduce quite a bit about a person from their appearance and body language. We can all think of a Tom or Mary we have known at some time who has died. If the recipient is in her 80s the medium is pretty safe in saying, 'I've got your mother coming through.' Of course, she might say, 'No, my mother's still alive and over a hundred' in which case the medium can say, 'It must be your grandmother then!'

I have heard so-called mediumship like this and it deserves the criticism that it gets, though in fairness the medium may genuinely be doing her best and she – I say 'she' because the majority of mediums are women – can only pass on as much as she is receiving. But a good medium will give evidence that can't be explained by cold reading, guesswork or any kind of gimmickry because it is so detailed and factual.

I shall give just one example. At a demonstration which I attended at the Stantonbury Theatre in Milton Keynes, Keith Charles, one of the mediums featured in my last book, gave a message to a boy in the audience named Paul, from a friend who had been killed in a road accident. Keith correctly gave the friend's name, Richard, and described how he died and the time of death. He added that Richard was telling him that Paul was planning to have a tattoo done of a cartoon character.

'That's right,' Paul agreed. 'I was going to have a wizard done!'

I would not call such a message trivial, and I defy any magician who boasts he can do what mediums do to come up with information of this sort by psychology and guesswork.

Mediums are often unfairly treated by the media. I would say, from my experience, that radio is more fair-minded in its approach than television. At all my interviews I was treated with courtesy, given the opportunity to put my point of view across and not made to feel like some kind of freak.

Indeed, some radio presenters and disc jockeys are very sympathetic and interested in the subject, making a point of inviting mediums and psychics onto their programmes. Derek Jameson, for example, is on record as saying that he supports mediums and what they do. Johnnie Walker, who interviewed me on Radio Five, told me that he was a hundred per cent convinced of life after death. Pete Murray also shares this belief. I remember several years ago he appeared on the platform of a meeting taken by Doris Collins at the Wimbledon Town Hall, where he spoke movingly of how Doris had helped him after the tragic death of his son.

Television producers seem on the whole to be less well disposed, although there are some notable exceptions. Plays, comedies and dramas still present caricatures of mediums in the Madame Arcati style. Where more favourable programmes are shown, they tend to be screened either first thing in the morning or in the middle of the night.

But the most virulent opposition comes from a small band of what might be termed professional sceptics, who make it their business to debunk anything psychic or paranormal. Some of these belong to CICOPS, the Committee for the Scientific Investigation of Claims of the Paranormal.

Members of CICOPS come in two varieties; those who, while suspicious of psychics, are prepared to listen to what they have to say, and the die hard sceptics who are not prepared to give an inch. One of the die hard variety, David Fisher, writing in their journal *The Skeptic*, puts forward the view that paranormal claims should be 'unceasingly ridiculed, caricatured and subjected to uncompromising criticism' – an attitude which is hardly scientific or objective.

Fortunately, however, there are researchers and writers such as Brian Inglis, Colin Wilson, Guy Lyon Playfair and the late D. Scott Rogo, whose books I recommend because they present the case fairly. Colin Wilson, in an interview with *Psychic News* stated, 'When the evidence is studied, there can be no doubt whatsoever of the reality of life after death.'

But if the evidence is so good, it may be asked, why isn't it generally accepted? There are several reasons for this. Firstly, we live in a materialistic society. The vast majority of people have been brought up with the idea that nothing exists beyond that which they can see, hear or touch. They are unable to conceive of anything beyond this so the facts are dismissed without even being considered. Those who take a different view are labelled as freaks or cranks. Science is firmly entrenched in this materialism, and scientists who should, by the nature of their profession, be open-minded, often have the most closed minds of all and hate to have their neatly worked out theories upset. There is also, quite understandably, a general fear of death and the majority of people would rather not think about it at all.

But we all have to die eventually, and I myself am convinced beyond any doubt that we do survive. My conviction is based not just on the evidence from the past, strong though that is, but on my experience of the twenty years I have spent in the Spiritualist movement. I do not think that anyone could be around mediums for so long without concluding that communication is a fact. And of course, the final proof to me is my own work as a medium, seeing and hearing the spirit people and knowing them to be as real as people on this earth.

'Well, I'd be a lot more impressed,' one reader of my book remarked, 'if your spirits could tell me something useful, like who's going to win the Grand National.'

It doesn't work like that – just as well, perhaps, since it would be open to abuse. And if they did tell me, I wouldn't necessarily trust them to get it right. I remember the cautionary tale of the man at the races, who heard a voice whisper in his ear, 'Put five pounds on Black Prince in the two o'clock.'

The man did so, and it won.

'Put ten pounds on Rob Roy in the three o'clock,' the voice urged.

Again, he obeyed, and again the horse won.

Excitedly, the voice whispered again, 'Put it all on Black Beauty in the 4.30.'

He did – and lost the lot.

'Damn!' said the voice.

2   In the News

For anyone who wants to find out more about Spiritualism, the *Psychic News* is a good place to start. It carries reports on the activities of mediums and healers all over the country as well as stories of psychic happenings and strange events.

I first came across this intriguing newspaper in a newsagents, long before I became involved in mediumship. The headline caught my eye. A famous actor – I forget which one – had just died. While the other papers were reporting on his funeral, the *Psychic News* was confidently announcing his spirit return. I became a regular reader and some years later, after I had joined the Spiritualist church of Wimbledon, began to contribute articles myself.

The paper's offices are situated in Museum Street, just near the British Museum, below their own Atlantis Bookshop which carries a wide range of books from psychical research and the paranormal to astrology and magic. On one of my visits to the then editor, Tony Ortzen, I asked him if he had always been a believer in life after death. He told me that he had always had a vague interest in the subject, but he had no idea when he began his career in journalism that he would end up working for a psychic newspaper. His involvement came about in a strange way.

It began when he was researching an article on the paranormal for the Buckinghamshire newspaper for which he was a reporter. He wrote to the *Psychic News* asking for information and they in turn featured his article in the paper. Not long afterwards he moved to London looking for work. He was offered three jobs on the same day; one with an oil company, one with an employment agency and one as a reporter on the *Psychic News*.

'It was the worst paid of all the jobs,' he told me, 'and the one with the worst prospects – but I knew without doubt that I would take it.'

In time he was promoted to assistant editor but he had no ambition to take over the paper. He had other, very different plans for his life – he intended to emigrate to Australia.

One Friday evening in 1981 he went home from the office feeling very uneasy. Maurice Barbanell, the editor, had returned from a holiday complaining of a slight chest infection. It didn't appear to be anything serious. Barbie, as he was affectionately known, was never ill, but Tony, although he didn't consider himself psychic in the normal way, had a strong presentiment that Barbie wouldn't be coming back. He was right. That night the phone rang. It was a friend of Barbie's, telling him that the editor had died.

Tony was in a dilemma. His travel arrangements had already been made, his house sold and his suitcases packed, but there was no one else who could take over the paper. He stepped into Barbanell's shoes and held the job for ten years before handing over the reins to the present editor, Tim Haigh.

I asked Tony whether he ever felt the ghosts of former editors peering over his shoulder when he was working. Barbanell had been a great influence on his life, a friend as well as an employer. He told me that he had done so on occasions, particularly when he first took over.

'There was one time when I had a particuarly difficult problem concerning the paper. I was sitting in Barbie's chair thinking about him. I had an overwhelmingly strong sense that he was in the room. I could even smell his cigar. He didn't say anything but soon after that the problem somehow solved itself.'

After his years of experience in the psychic field, Tony has no doubts about life after death. 'No one piece of evidence is convincing on its own,' he admits, 'but it's the accumulation of evidence, from many sources, over many years, that makes the case so strong.' But he added, 'Proof is a very personal matter. People have to find their own evidence. Other people's experiences are never enough. The evidence may not be dramatic, but it means a lot to the person themselves. It can literally change their lives.'

Tim Haigh also had an interesting story to relate about how he came to work for the paper. He was brought up in a Spiritualist family so the idea of life after death was not strange to him. His parents often had sittings with mediums who visited the house. He and his brother would stand at the top of the stairs listening to the sound of Red Indian voices booming out from mediums in trance.

'I used to hate it,' he admitted. 'I rebelled against it.'

Then, at the age of sixteen, his views changed and he began to take an interest in the subject. After leaving school he took a degree in business studies followed by a post-graduate course in printing and publishing. He didn't know what he wanted to do by way of a career except that he had a vague idea that he wanted to do something in the psychic field, possibly working in a bookshop.

With this in mind, he spent several days traipsing around London looking for a job. One day he called in at the *Psychic News* bookshop, which was then in Earlham Street, off Charing Cross Road, in order to pick up a book his mother had asked him to collect. On the way out of the shop his eye was caught by a copy of the paper lying on the floor, which featured an advertisement for a job as assistant in the shop. He made enquiries and was told that the vacancy had already been filled. However, there was another job going with the paper, as assistant to the advertising manager.

He was conducted up the stairs to the Dickensian offices above to meet Tony Ortzen. Ten minutes later he had been given the job. Shortly afterwards, he was promoted to advertising manager then, on Tony's resignation, to editor.

Tim has many plans for the future of the paper. 'I'd like to include more first-hand reports of events, rather than relying so much on stories our readers send in. I'd also like to expand our overseas links. There are a lot of exciting developments taking place now, particularly in Australia and New Zealand. And I want to give more prominence to the scientific investigation of the paranormal.'

He plans to extend the paper's editorial base to take in other subjects in this field, but he adds, 'We are first and foremost a Spiritualist newspaper and we will always remain so. We aim to present Spiritualism in a way that makes people want to look into it for themselves.'

A name which has appeared in the *Psychic News* is Stephen O'Brien. Since the publication of his first bestselling books, *Visions of Another World* and *Voices from Heaven*, Stephen has become without doubt Britain's leading medium. Though just thirty-seven years old, he has appeared at city halls and theatres all over the country several times, and has often been seen on prime time BBC and ITV. Programmes include *Gloria Live* with Gloria Hunniford, *Daytime UK* with Judi Spiers, and a three hour live debate about the paranormal on Channel 4's *After Dark*.

On Gloria Hunniford's show the British public passed judgement on his mediumship when they were asked, 'Can Stephen O'Brien contact the spirit world: Yes or No?' The BBC phone lines immediately jammed, and in less than twenty minutes 8,000 calls flooded the studios – seven calls per second – resulting in overwhelming support of his gifts. Eighty-two per cent voted yes.

There was an unexpected drama on Granada Television's *This Morning* programme when a live telephone call accused Stephen of worshipping 'a different God to the Christians'. The medium instantly replied with gentle authority, 'There is only *one* God,' at which point all IBA channels across Britain lost sound and vision for four minutes. Technicians were baffled by the national power failure and were subsequently unable to account for it. Next day, with tongue-in-cheek, the *Daily Star* reported: 'Medium Steve spooks up the TV works.'

I asked Stephen about the problems involved when working live on television. 'It's always a hazardous undertaking,' he said, 'because mediums must contend with cameras, bright lights, and studio audiences who seek entertainment instead of reverent contact with another world. It's also quite a task to cope with knowing your work is being watched and judged by millions of people. On reflection, I don't think TV studios provide the right conditions in which to demonstrate mediumship correctly.'

Stephen's appearance on *Wogan* illustrates his point. Though he had demonstrated his gifts quite successfully on channels such as Ulster TV and Central, this programme was a particularly harrowing experience for him.

His interview with Terry Wogan went smoothly enough but when asked to demonstrate to the studio audience, the woman to whom he went with a message was unable to accept anything he said. Regarding it as a humiliating experience in front of 10 million people, Stephen confessed to me that when the show was over, he had groaned to the producers, 'Just dig a hole and bury me in it!'

However, it later emerged that the message, which he had felt to be so right, *had* been correct after all. A College of Higher Education lecturer from Cambridgeshire, Mrs Judy Brewer, had been seated in the television theatre audience and had understood it all but had been too shy to speak up. The studio staff had previously seen a woman waving her hand to attract Stephen's attention during his spirit message, but he had been dazzled by a much too bright follow-spot, trained on him during transmission.

Mrs Brewer, who was there with her family as part of a birthday treat, confirmed every detail: the names and facts relayed were all placed by her, especially an earring Stephen had mentioned. Through the medium, the communicator (Mrs Brewer's spirit father) mentioned someone had been looking for an earring in a jewellery box. They found one, but couldn't find the other.

In a personal letter sent to Terry Wogan of which copies were also sent to Stephen and the BBC, she recounted that on her way to work that very morning she had forgotten to put on some earrings and called at her swimming club to ask the attendant if they had a lost property box so that she could borrow a pair. He promptly produced a jewellery box, and in it Mrs Brewer found one of her own mislaid earrings! 'It was still in my pocket at the show,' she wrote.

Stephen commented to me, 'Can you image the electric effect it would have had on the nation, had she produced the earring on camera? No doubt that was what the spirit people wanted.'

Mrs Brewer expressed her willingness to be a guest on the programme to fully explain the impact of the message to the millions of viewers, but the BBC said their schedules wouldn't permit this. Stephen, quite naturally, was unhappy with their decision, but he said, 'At least Terry Wogan extended another invitation to appear at some future date.'

Stephen also points out how easy it is to criticize spirit messages and dismiss them as trivial. 'It's precisely this kind of personal detail that can be so meaningful and convincing to investigators. The *Wogan* link contained facts which made the recipient say 'How on earth could the medium have known that?'

He also maintains that the only people who can judge the true value of spirit evidence are the two people involved: the person on the other side sending the message, and the one in this world, receiving it. 'It's often the small, intimate memories that really hit home; people are frequently amazed, or so moved that they burst into tears.'

To consolidate this viewpoint, he told me of a further example, about a message he gave to a woman whose husband had recently died. Stephen relayed the man's name then added, 'He says I'm to tell you about the black rosary beads with the crucifix attached.'

Instantly, the woman became very emotional. Through tears, she informed the audience that she was a devout Roman Catholic but her husband had been an atheist. As he lay unconscious and dying of cancer she had been anxious about the fate of his soul, and so at his last breath she had said a prayer for him, pressing into his hand the black rosary beads and crucifix. 'Your message has done three things,' the elated woman told Stephen. 'It's brought me comfort, confirmed that my husband knew what I'd done, and also proved his survival beyond death.'

Another seemingly innocent statement from spirit caused a similar reaction at a large Leicester meeting, when Stephen was contacted by a boy called Peter who had been killed in a car accident. The boy's mother, who was sitting in the gallery, acknowledged the name and came forward to the microphone.

'He keeps saying 'Jean,'' Stephen said. Then he quickly corrected himself. 'No, its "jeans" with an "s".'

The astonished woman burst into tears and told the crowd that her brother, the boy's uncle, had put Peter's favourite pair of jeans into the coffin with him. Furthermore, the brother was seated a few rows behind her and had been too shy to come forward. 'You've changed my life and given me hope,' the woman told Stephen, and she hugged him during his autograph signing session at the end of the evening.

Stephen's theatre meetings at some of the country's most prestigious venues, including the world famous City Varieties Music Hall in Leeds, have made him into something of a star, but he has mixed feelings about being seen as part of the world of showbusiness. 'Hopefully my meetings are enjoyable, and they do allow me to reach people who wouldn't otherwise hear the great news of life after death, but I'm not there to provide an entertainment. I think of my evenings as spiritual experiences, and my work as a service to mankind.'

However, this increased publicity has dramatically changed

his life. He now receives stacks of letters each week: following major television, radio or mass-circulation magazine features – such as in *Woman*, *Essentials* and *Chat* – this can escalate to about 300, arriving from several parts of the world. Stephen answers each one personally because, 'if people take the trouble to write, they deserve a reply.' But he admits this is fast becoming an impossible task and he's now contemplating the services of a secretary.

Of his many followers he commented to me, 'People say it must be wonderful to have the love of the public, but it's a very strange, distant kind of affection. People respond to my mediumship, and what it means to *them*, saying they feel they've known me all their lives, even though we've never actually met. But in reality, I'm still a very private man, and those who write don't know whether or not I can afford the next meal.'

He finds public recognition an anathema, and rarely goes out now. He cannot visit a Spiritualist church to enjoy the service as he likes to do without being mobbed.

'I was in London recently,' he told me, 'and my manager and I were driving to Wales when I took a wrong turning and stopped to ask directions from two men in boiler suits. One of them cheekily remarked: 'I thought *you* would have known, mate, with your voices!" Stephen coloured up red and drove away as quickly as possible.

'People behave very oddly towards celebrities, as if they *own* you,' he remarked, rather dumbfoundedly. 'Once, a strange looking woman chased me into a health food shop and wouldn't relent until I'd autographed her empty umbrella case!'

He still finds it hard to come to terms with his fame, guarding 'whatever little privacy I have left more fiercely than ever.' As a result, Stephen's home is his castle; callers are never admitted and no photographs of it or his possessions have ever been published. Media interviews are usually conducted in hotel coffee shops and restaurants.

Being called upon to face large numbers of strangers at each of his demonstrations, he is also more conscious now of the increased responsibility this brings. 'Often at my meetings there are a thousand or more people in the audience. Many have tremendous expectations of me, and hope is written across their foreheads. I always explain that mediumship is an experiment and that the mental and emotional conditions they create within the theatre can ruin or make communication successful – then I do my best to help them as much as I can.'

Stephen strongly believes that audiences generate a great deal of the psychic power needed by mediums to assist them in clearly communicating with the other side of life.

As well as yearly touring and dealing with his mountains of correspondence, he also has to find time for writing his regular monthly contributions to *Two Worlds* magazine and also the manuscripts for his autobiographies. His new book, *In Touch with Eternity* is the third volume of his life story and seems set to be another bestseller.

'Mediumship is a spiritual service to those who grieve, or seek comfort and enlightenment from worlds beyond earth,' he says. 'The life of a medium is never an easy one, and there's no glamour in it! In fact, it's very hard work. But at the end of the day, it's all worthwhile when someone writes to me or says just how much the quality of their life has improved because of a message from eternity.'

One of the most remarkable mediums to make the headlines in recent years has been Rosemary Brown, who claims to write music under the direction of some of the great composers of the past, including Liszt, Chopin and Beethoven.

Rosemary's music is known all over the world and she has given recitals at leading concert halls including the Wigmore Hall in London. She has won the support of a number of eminent musicians, including the pianist John Lill, who himself admits that he receives spirit inspiration. The late composer Humphrey Searle, who was an authority on Liszt, was an enthusiastic champion of her work. His verdict was, 'You couldn't fake music like this without years of training' – a significant comment since Rosemary's musical education has been very limited.

Professor Ian Parrott of the University of Wales, who made a special study of her music, was also convinced that she was genuinely in touch with the composers and that she captured their styles – a much more difficult feat than merely imitating them. He was particularly impressed by a piece dictated by Liszt called *Grubelei* describing it as 'the sort of thing Liszt might have written next, had he lived longer in this world.'

Rosemary is unique among mediums for the quality and range of her work but from time to time one does hear of composers claiming to receive inspiration from musicians in the world beyond. Such claims, of course, need to be treated with caution. However, it seems not unreasonable to assume that musicians whose work provided joy and upliftment to so many while they were on earth should continue to compose in the beyond, and should be able to inspire present-day musicians occasionally.

As a musician myself – I play the organ at Wimbledon Church – I was intrigued to see in *Psychic News* some years ago an article about a composer called Georgina Brazier-Potter, who claims to be inspired by Ivor Novello. Subsequently, we met and she told me about her work.

Georgina began her musical career early. At the age of ten she was a junior exhibitor at the Royal Academy of Music. She first began composing in 1965 but, although she was already interested in psychic matters, she had no idea that she was receiving help from the other side of life until she had sittings with a medium who told her that Novello was with her.

'I found it hard to believe at first,' she admitted. 'Why should such a famous composer take an interest in me?' She was, of course, familiar with Novello's better known songs and musicals but she had never seen him on stage in his lifetime. However, she became convinced when several other mediums also described him. One of them, the psychic artist Coral Polge, even drew his portrait, though Coral knew nothing about Georgina or her work.

Unlike Rosemary Brown, Georgina is not conscious of receiving inspiration while she is actually composing. It is only afterwards that Novello will make her aware that he has worked something from his own music into her compositions. Obviously, much of Novello's music is well-known, but she insists that the extracts she finds in her music, which range from two to six bars in length, are carefully woven in so that they are not easily recognizable as Novello's music and are from lesser known songs (usually the verses rather than the more familiar chorus). Over the past few years she has developed her psychic ability and Novello is able to contact her himself. She gave me an example:-

'I'd been to see Ivor's musical *Perchance to Dream* and was very taken with the love theme that links the scenes. I thought I'd get the score from the library and after I'd done so I "heard" Ivor say to me "have a look at your Kenwood House music," a piece I'd written some years before. When I did so, I was amazed to find that I had unknowingly worked the same theme into my music: the interesting parallel being that "Kenwood House" describes a stately home in Hampstead; "Huntersmoon" is the stately home featured in *Perchance to Dream*.'

Georgina also has sittings with the well-known medium Lee Lacy, who has given her additional proof.

'On one occasion, I wanted to read a particular biography of Ivor and asked the library to get me a copy. The same day I was impressed to walk down Marylebone High Street and, to my surprise, the book I wanted was in a shop window! I bought it. At my next sitting with Lee he said, "Ivor tells me you've bought a book about him and that there's something wrong with one of the pictures." Correct: the frontispiece photograph is upside down! Ivor also mentioned to Lee a spelling mistake on the Yeates-Hurlstone trophy award which hangs above my piano. When I got home I checked. I found the second 'e' was missing from 'Yeates': proof that the spirit people are often more observant than we are.'

Another composer from whom Georgina sometimes receives help is Elgar, but unlike Novello, he usually contacts her via Lee Lacy. She first became aware of his influence when she went to an exhibition about him in Hampstead, and saw a music manuscript containing bars from a very early composition, *Ave Verum*.

'I asked my library to find it. They had a hard job – it's a very obscure piece. However, they eventually did. When I looked at it carefully I found that I had used the same downward scale opening bars in my Hampstead piece, "Holly Place," which depicts Hampstead's Italian church, and is also in the style of an *Ave Verum*.'

Georgina has won many awards for her work. Movements of the Hampstead Suite – 'Hampstead Heath' and 'Kenwood House' have both won the Yeates-Hurlstone trophy. She has also won first prizes in the Brighton and Cornwall County music festivals and her 'Tribute to the Walmer Lifeboat' was premiered by the Deal Symphony Orchestra in 1987.

I asked her why Novello and Elgar chose to work with her rather than with a well-established composer. She feels it is because she is able to be in tune with them (no pun intended).

'Ivor says that, through working with me, he has the opportunity of using his music in a different way, rather than – as he did when he was here – writing songs mainly for the stage and commercial market. Also of course, it's his way of proving survival after death. He is now working with me in a different way, i.c., on arrangements of his Chinese Temple theme from *Careless Rapture*. He also wants me to reshape certain movements of *Valley of Song*, a musical he left unfinished at the time of his death. Elgar and Ivor are currently collaborating on a song I am writing called "Somebody Cares" (Elgar is involved with the harmony, Ivor with the melody). So my work with them both is very much an on-going thing.'

This wish to prove to the world that they survive seems to be shared by Rosemary Brown's composers also. In the words of Liszt, 'The threat of life does not end at death. It is merely transferred to another spool.'

Musical mediumship is a very rare gift, and so is psychic art. For many years Coral Polge has been Britain's leading exponent in this field. However, psychic art is now becoming more popular and there are a number of new artists who are starting to make a name for themselves.

Rita Taylor has actually been drawing spirit people for many years, but it is only recently that her name has become well-known, due mainly to an article about her which appeared in the *Daily Star*.

Many mediums I have spoken to have discovered their psychic gifts following a period of trauma in their own lives, and this was the case with Rita. She was in her twenties and had three young children, one of whom was seriously ill. Several mediums had told her that she had the potential for psychic art but, because of her family situation, she had done nothing about it. However, she became friendly with the healer to whom she used to take her son for treatment. One day not long after her son's tragic death at the age of eight, she felt inspired to draw for the healer a picture of a child. The healer recognized the face at once. It was another young boy to whom she had given healing, who had since died.

Encouraged by this, Rita joined a development circle, then, some time later, began working in public. She now travels all over the country and abroad and is much in demand wherever she goes. Unlike Coral who had some art training when she was

young, Rita has never had any formal instruction in drawing.
Her method of working is similar to Coral's however, in that
neither of them 'sees' the people they are sketching. Rita
explained to me, 'I just allow my hand to be guided. I never
know what I am going to draw until I see the face starting to
appear on the paper.'

One of the drawings of which Rita is most proud is of a boy
called Bobbie. Bobbie had been just seventeen when he was
killed in a collision with a police car. His mother was unable to
come to terms with his death and her priest – showing an
unusual open-mindedness in a clergyman – suggested that she
had a sitting with Rita.

Rita's portrait was an exact likeness. The sitting brought
immense comfort to the mother and completely changed her
outlook on life. She and Bobbie's father now run their own
healing sanctuary.

Stories such as this show how remarkable mediumship can be
and challenge any sceptic to explain it away by any alternative
explanation. And I cannot resist adding here a couple of the
most extraordinary stories of mediumship I have ever come
across. They were told to me by Alan Law, who is the treasurer
of Wimbledon Spiritualist Church, and who has worked as a
medium and healer for some thirty years.

Alan has had a varied career. He was for some years a
professional footballer and has also worked with a Formula One
motor racing team. Not the sort of occupations one would
associate with a medium, but then, contrary to popular
impression, mediums are not airy-fairy people with their heads
in the clouds.

Alan lived for some time in Italy, where he was well-known
locally as a medium. It was during this time that he became
conscious of the presence of the spirit of a woman who seemed
to have attached herself to him. She was able to communicate
quite clearly with him and told him that her name was Kresenzia
and that she had died in 1949 of leukaemia. But their
communication was by thought – she spoke a language Alan
didn't understand and couldn't recognize. There was a man
with her who wore the spiked helmet of a Prussian officer and
whose name, he knew, was Ladislaus. Yet Alan had no idea who
either of them were or why they were with him.

He made enquiries, but no one had heard of the dead couple.

Eighteen months passed. Then one day he was sent by the Fiat company, for whom he worked, to another town to give English lessons to some of their senior executives.

One of his pupils was a lady named Wilma. As soon as he saw her, Alan knew instinctively that the mysterious couple belonged to her. After the lesson, he invited her to have coffee with him, when he cautiously broached the subject.

Wilma knew the names. Kresenzia was her mother and Ladislaus her father. She identified the language they spoke as the Swiss-German dialect of the district where they had lived. She was very suspicious as to how Alan had come by this information and for a while was quite convinced that he was a witch! Eventually, however, she came to accept his mediumship. When he returned to England she came with him, and they have been together now for ten years.

The second incident Alan described to me took place when he was living in London (long before he went to Italy and met Wilma). He was driving along on his way to meet his girlfriend when he passed a Spiritualist Church and noticed an advertisement for a meeting that evening which was being taken by a medium from Nottingham, George Daisley. This was someone he had always wanted to see and he regretted that he wouldn't be able to go. However, when he got to the station where he and his girlfriend had arranged to meet he was told by the station-master that she had phoned to say that she wasn't coming as she had been delayed at work. Not too disappointed, Alan decided to go to the meeting instead.

He arrived at the church late and sat at the back. When the meeting opened the chairman apologized to the audience, saying that George Daisley had had a mild heart attack that afternoon and would not be able to work. He had come to the church but he wouldn't be giving a demonstration – another medium was going to stand in for him.

Daisley himself then came onto the platform and made his apologies but added that there was one message he had to give.

'When I entered the church this afternoon,' he said, 'a young RAF boy made contact with me who wanted to speak to someone in the audience. This boy is desperate to get a message to his mother.' And he told Alan that the boy wanted to speak to him.

Alan denied that he knew anyone in the Air Force, but the

medium was insistent. He said that the boy, whom he named as Oliver Ashton, had died when his plane crashed. He had been outside England but not over enemy territory. He gave the time and date of his death as 12.15 on 13th March 1945 and also gave eight names which he claimed were the other members of the crew. The boy, he said, was concerned that his mother was trying to raise money to bring his remains back to England. He described the boy's mother's home and told Alan that he would be going there.

'You'll be taken into the dining-room, where you'll find there is a piano and on the piano are photographs of the boy, his sister and his mother and father.' He ended by saying that Oliver had met Alan, but only once.

It took Alan three years to trace the boy. He went to see his grandmother who lived in Liverpool and asked her if she knew of anyone in the family called Oliver Ashton. His grandmother recalled a cousin of his father's known in the family as Dolly Smith, saying that she had remarried and she had an idea that her married name was Ashton. She had had a son called Oliver who had been killed in the war.

Alan got Dolly Ashton's address and went to visit her. She was surprised to see him. 'Come into the dining-room,' she invited. 'I won't take you into the sitting-room because it's cold in there.'

He followed her in, and found the piano with the photographs on it as Daisley had described. When he had told her the story she went upstairs and came down with a photograph and a wrist-watch. The watch, which had belonged to her son, had stopped at 12.20 on the 13th March, and the photo showed the other members of his crew, whose names tallied with the names Daisley had given. She confirmed that the plane had crashed over Ireland on a training flight and she had indeed been saving up money to bring his body back.

Oliver had, she said, seen Alan just once. He had visited Alan's mother in hospital a few days after his birth, which explained why Alan didn't remember anything about it!

3   'I Have Only Slipped Away'

It is said that we live in a materialistic age, yet there are very few people who have not, at some time in their lives, had an encounter with the supernatural – even though some of them would die rather than admit it! When I was compiling this book I put an appeal in the press inviting people to write to me about their psychic experiences. The response was so great that I couldn't reply to all the letters. Several of them mentioned Doris Stokes. Although it is some years since she died, she is still remembered with affection as the most famous medium of recent times.

Geoff Nunn told me a remarkable story. His father was taken ill in 1982. He was admitted to hospital several times, each time making a good recovery. Then he suffered a stroke, following which he went into a coma. This time the doctors held out little hope. Geoff, his mother and his brothers all feared the worst.

Geoff had no particular interest in Spiritualism at that time, but he saw a Doris Stokes meeting advertised and, out of curiosity, went in, sitting as far back as possible.

> About half-way through the meeting she said she wanted to come to someone near the back called Nunn. I put my hand up and she gave me a flawless description of my father's father, including some details that were only known to the two of us and not to the family. She then went on to say that the reason I was at the meeting was because of my father. She described all his health problems and said that he was in a coma, adding that on the third day of the following month he would come out of the coma and be with us for a few more years yet.

Doris added that Geoff would find a development circle and develop his own mediumistic ability – all of her predictions came true.

More of Geoff's story later. Jennifer Trodd of Hampshire received an unexpected communication from her grandfather whom she had never met. The medium said there was a tall man there who had what appeared to be a wart on the palm of his hand. He said something about naval tailoring and mentioned a Landguard Road. None of this meant anything to Jennifer so she went and checked with her father.

'Who on earth have you been talking to?' her father asked. 'That's my father. He used to do naval tailoring in Landguard Road in Portsmouth and that wart-like blister he had on his hand was caused by an infection he caught in earlier days when he used to work in a tannery.'

Animals also survive death and often come back to their owners. Jennifer was very upset when her fox terrier, Waggles, was killed in a road accident. She appealed to her other grandfather, who had died when she was twenty-one, 'If there is an afterlife, please let me know and please find my Waggles for me.' Some time later she went to see a medium, a Mr Roberts, who spoke of her grandfather and how she had placed fresias by his face as he lay in his coffin.

> As the medium Mr Roberts was telling me these things I saw a bright white light coming from him to me. In that moment, he described my little dog, saying she had her paws on my lap looking up at me. He then said she ran to his fireplace and picked up the pieces of coal which had fallen on the grate. 'She is playing with them,' he said, 'throwing them in the air and dropping them at your feet and watching you.' This was fantastic evidence, as she always got a stone when I took her out and dropped it at my feet for me to throw for her. If I threw that stone into a lot of shingle she would always come back with the same stone that I had thrown.

A lady from Portsmouth told me how a spirit voice saved her from a fire.

> It happened at a time when my husband worked nights. I was alone with my two daughters who were asleep in bed. I had just sat down to watch television when I felt as if someone was giving me a clear set of instructions which went like this. 'Go into your bedroom, pull the bed away from the wall and look behind the bed.' At first I shrugged this off and continued watching

television, but the instructions came again and again and continued with such a feeling of urgency that I was compelled to respond. I went into my bedroom, looked behind the bed and found to my astonishment that there was an electrical fault and my carpet had just caught fire!

There were a few ghost stories, like the one sent to me by Joyce Barnard from Sussex:

I was seventeen and was working as a land girl. One evening in late summer I was coming back to the farm after a long walk, and stopped in the tractor shed. It was one of the older parts of the farm and was built of red brick. The low evening sun shone into the building, and I stepped in to look at some initials scratched into the brickwork. I wondered what sort of life the people who had made these marks had led, whether they wore boots, or went barefoot, etc.

As I stood there, feeling very nostalgic, I was joined by an elderly man. He wore corduroy trousers, strapped up under his knees. He had a 'pork-pie' hat, and over his shirt a waistcoat and a wide, brass-buckled belt. He told me that he had driven the first tractor in these parts, and people had come from the next village to see it.

I turned to the initials scratched on the wall, and asked if he knew whose they were, but when I looked to him for an answer, he had gone.

The following day, I asked the farm manager, a Mr Kemp, who the old man was, and described his rather old-fashioned clothes. Mr Kemp looked at me rather sharply and asked if I believed in ghosts. I said 'No, of course I don't.' 'Well, you do now' he told me. 'That was (I've forgotten the name after so long) and he's been dead two years.'

It is sometimes said in Spiritualist circles that no one can come back and communicate until at least a week after their death. In my experience, this is not true. I have known people to come back within a day or two, or even within hours. A friend of mine went to a church the day after his father's death. The medium on that occasion was Lee Lacy. Lee made a contact with his father at once, describing him accurately.

'This man isn't even buried yet,' he exclaimed, then added, 'he's telling you to put the fish up in front' – an apparently nonsensical remark, until I explain that my friend's father had been a keen fisherman and one of the wreaths had been made in the shape of a fish.

Irene Newell wrote to me about her close friend, May, who was killed in a car crash:

> Her death was on the Friday. Two days later, on the Sunday, I went to the local Spiritualist church and sat in my usual place. I was the first to get a message. The medium (whom I did not know) came to me and said 'I have a lady here who has only very recently passed. She is radiant, and wants you to know that she is so sorry, for your sake, that it was so sudden. She is alright and so very happy. she brings you lots of love – and she is saying her name is May.' I could hardly believe my ears. I couldn't wait for the service to end to get out of the church, the tears pouring down my face. Since then, I have had many messages of love, help and guidance from my beloved friend.

Often, after a person has died, those who were close to them continue to feel their presence around in the house. I was very conscious of this when my father died. I would feel him standing behind me and turn round, but there would be no one there. Sometimes I thought I caught a glimpse of him out of the corner of my eye but, when I turned my head to look, he had vanished.

Experiences like this are very common. They take various forms; small sounds, the whiff of a familiar scent, a touch of a hand on the shoulder. These things are usually dismissed as imagination. Of course, we shouldn't get into the habit of attributing every unexplained noise to spirits; it is as well to look for a natural explanation first. I am reminded of the story of the woman who was convinced that the antique sofa she had purchased was haunted, because every time she sat on it she heard the sound of deep breathing. Then her father investigated – and found a hedgehog hibernating inside!

But sometimes there is no physical explanation. Those who have died often remain close to their homes and families for a while, trying to make that presence felt and to reassure those they love that they are still alive. Some people find this comforting but others are frightened by it.

'Two days after my father died,' one lady told me, 'I saw him standing at the top of the stairs. I was so terrified I ran out of the house and slammed the door.' She then found herself locked out, and had to get a neighbour to climb through a window and let her in! I pointed out the illogicality of her reaction.

'You wouldn't have been afraid of your father when he was alive. Why should you be afraid of him now?'

She agreed with me, and promised not to run away if she should see him again. Of course, her fear was perfectly understandable, but once she had accepted her father's presence as natural, and realized that he was still the same person she had known and not a ghost, she was able to come to terms with it. She never saw him as clearly again but she continued to be aware of him from time to time and derived great comfort from knowing that he hadn't gone very far away.

Winifred Cox's story was typical of many I received. Her husband died very suddenly of a heart attack. One night soon afterwards, when she was sitting alone, she saw him.

> It was a strange sighting, like a small picture, and it was gone in a split second. When I turned my head to look, it had vanished. That night, when I went to bed, I said 'goodnight' to his photo, as I always did. I might have fallen into a light sleep, but I was not dreaming, when I heard a voice, so loud it startled me. 'Goodnight, Win,' it said. I was convinced that my son, Tony, had friends in the house and that one of them had called out to me as he was leaving, so I got up to look but there was no one there. The house was empty.
>
> I had heard stories about mediums and thought maybe I should go and satisfy this feeling of wanting to know more. In the paper shop was a Spiritualist newspaper. It mentioned the Spiritualist Association in Belgrave Square so I rang them up and made an appointment.
>
> The medium was a motherly lady who put me at my ease. We sat for a few moments before she said, 'I have your husband. He is saying you must see about your arm.' I knew I had arthritis, as a doctor had told me, but the pain was getting worse so after this advice, I went to see another doctor who sent me to Queen Mary's Hospital, where they discovered I had a trapped nerve. Later, I had an operation to remove it.

It is in such ways as this that those in the next world demonstrate their continuing care for us. They are not all-knowing, but they can see a little further than we can and, given the opportunity, they will help us just as they would have done when they were alive.

Geoff Nunn, whose message from Doris Stokes I recounted earlier, experienced a strange phenomenon in his house when his father died some years later. The death happened at 3.10 in the afternoon. At 10.30 that evening Geoff was about to go to bed when the smoke alarm near his bedroom started to ring for no apparent reason:

> I took the alarm off the wall mount and waved it to and fro but to no avail, so I finally took the battery out. The next day I met my mother and brothers and mentioned this to them. They told me they had experienced unusual phenomena as well. My eldest brother, Stephen, said that, at exactly midnight, his radio alarm, which is always set to 6 a.m. switched itself on and played out at full volume. He tried to stop it by pressing various buttons but it continued to play and he had to unplug it. My next eldest brother, Richard, said that at 4.10 a.m. (exactly thirteen hours after my father's passing) his answerphone had played by itself without anyone phoning him, whilst at my mother's house we all noticed that the video recorder clock was stuck at 3.10 p.m! I had been given my father's watch and, as a gesture to him, I wore it to the next church service I attended. The service finished at 8.30 but when I glanced at the watch it was stuck at 3.10. A watch repairer said there was nothing wrong with it!

The death of a child is always tragic and I was very moved by the letter I received from Elizabeth Cole about her daughter.

> Twenty six years ago (on the 25th February) I lost a beautiful seventeen year old daughter with leukaemia. She was ill for nearly a year and during that time I picked up a book in the library called *Beyond the Horizon* by Grace Rosher. It was the first psychic book I had ever read and it certainly changed my way of thinking. As I read it I could hardly believe it was true and yet it seemed to give me hope. One part of me wanted to believe it but another part kept saying it was too good to be true. I kept putting the book down and picking it up again. My daughter, whose name was Patricia, said, 'What on earth are you reading, Mum?' and I replied, 'This is a very queer book. According to this, in the next world there are houses and trees and flowers. If that is what it's like I wouldn't mind going there, would you?' And she said, 'I certainly wouldn't.' She had no idea she had a fatal illness but of

course I knew, although I never gave up hoping she would be healed. When Patricia died I bought this wonderful book and when I read it again I believed it but I was not 100% sure.

Three months after Patricia's death, Mrs Cole went to see the famous medium Ena Twig:

For a whole hour my daughter communicated with me. One of the first things she said was, 'I am very happy and I shall be happier still when you stop grieving.' Once I knew she was alive and happy and continuing with her studies I found it quite easy to stop grieving.

I shall always remember the joy that filled my heart when I realized she was alive. I came out of Mrs Twigg's house floating on air and I remember how I wanted to dance down the road. When I got to the Greenline bus I had to restrain myself from shouting out loud to the other passengers, 'My daughter, who I thought was dead, is alive!' Since that happy day I have done my very best to spread the truth.'

Children are often psychic and some of them could teach adults a thing or two in their easy acceptance of the presences of spirit people around them. Lesley Hammerton's little boy has the makings of a medium, to judge by her letter.

A couple of weeks ago Eddie came to me and said 'Mummy's dead!' I asked him whose Mummy and he told me 'Your Mummy.' My Mum has been dead now for 15 years. Eddie knew this but had never bothered much about it. I had only ever shown him a picture of her. For a couple of days he would keep on about 'Mummy's dead.' Then the other night he came down the stairs and said 'Your Mummy said I'm a good boy.' Then he went back to bed again, quite happy. The next day I asked him about this and he said he had seen my Mummy. I asked what she looked like, and he told me she had black hair which was true, but any dark hair to Eddie is black, so I didn't make too much of it. It was when I asked him what colour eyes did she have that shocked me. He told me 'her eyes are green,' which was true, but Eddie couldn't have seen this from her picture as it's in black and white.

Bill Salter told me of a sitting with Leslie Flint. Leslie, who has now retired, has the very rare gift known as 'direct voice'. This means that the spirit voices can be heard by the sitters themselves, and do not come from Leslie's vocal chords, as scientific tests have proved. Bill played me a tape of the sitting, which took place a few months after his wife Rose had died. Her voice was faint but, to Bill, instantly recognizable.

'Hello, Bill how are you?'

'Take your time,' Bill encouraged her, sensing the difficulty she was having in speaking.

'I'm all right now.' The voice grew a little stronger. 'You were right,' she added, referring to Bill's belief in life after death, which she had not shared while on earth. 'I can't take it in. I'm sorry for all the trouble.'

'You would have done the same for me,' Bill responded, thinking of how he had nursed her while she was ill.

'You can't keep all that stuff of mine,' Rose went on. 'It clutters the place up. Get rid of it. What are you going to do with yourself? Are you going away? I know you've been talking about a coach trip. Has he got a cold?' she asked, meaning the medium. 'No colds here. It all seems so strange. I remember sleeping and waking up and seeing people and places. I must have been coming and going ... I've met all my people. I didn't suffer all that much. I was in a sort of dream world.'

Rose promised to come back to help Bill with his psychic work and with that her voice faded. Listening to the tape, I felt as if I was eavesdropping onto an intimate private conversation, such as any husband and wife might have who had been apart for a while. The words were so ordinary, yet to Bill they meant so much. And this is my answer to those who claim that communications are trivial. Yes, it has to be admitted that they seldom contain earth shattering revelations, but their very simplicity gives them the ring of truth.

Eileen Rouse and her husband made a pact that whichever of them died first would try to come back and communicate with the survivor. To prove their identity, they chose a word, 'Timmy,' which was the name of their cat. Eileen's husband died of a heart attack and, soon afterwards, she went to see a medium. The following extracts come from her booklet, *A Promise Fulfilled.*

* * *

Near the end of the sitting he said, 'The person you have lost died very quickly, to do with the heart, but you are not to go on suffering. He wants you to be happy and find someone better.' I said my husband would not say that. He loved me and would not want me to find anyone else. The medium sat very still for a moment then he said, 'Tim … Tim … Timmy.' I swear no one other than myself knew what we had agreed as our password. When I had said, 'That is not my husband' he had replied with the only way I would know for sure that it was him.

It was not long before Eileen's husband began to make his presence known around the house. She was indoors with her family when some relations arrived.

We were just going to have tea when we heard an alarm going off. It was faint so we thought it must be next door, but it seemed a funny time to set an alarm for. Next day was Saturday and all the family came again, including my son who had not been the day before. At exactly 12.30 the alarm we had heard the previous evening went off again. My son said, 'That's Dad's alarm on his watch!' He got up and lifted the lid off the container where I had put it and, sure enough, it was the alarm going. I had not set or rewound the watch since my husband had worn it.

Many other things happened. Tapping noises were heard on the tables. Doors opened and closed. A light bulb fell out of its holder and, when she went to put in a new bulb she found that the socket, that had been faulty before, was now perfectly all right. None of this frightened her, since she knew it was her husband who was responsible. She received messages from a number of different mediums, one of whom was Marie Wakeling. Marie produced a most unlikely sounding piece of evidence:

'I don't know if this makes sense to you,' she said, 'but he's talking about a dolphin and says its name is Sammy.' This was really unbelievable, because in the August before my husband died I had said I would like a dolphin, so he got a piece of wood and had spent three days carving and polishing it. When he had finished it I put it on the shelf and said, 'I will call him Sammy the dolphin.'

I have not included these stories because they provide dramatic evidence of life after death – on the contrary, most of them might be completely unconvincing to a sceptic. What they do illustrate is how making spiritual contact with someone who has died and receiving reassurances that they have survived has such a great effect on people's lives. Of course, no medium can take away the pain of loss. We all grieve when we lose someone near to us, but if we can be sure that they live on, that they are still close, then death loses its terrible finality.

I have seen many lives transformed by experiences such as these. They give an inner conviction that cannot be taken away. The period of grief then becomes, in a strange way, a blessing in disguise. It makes us look within and discover a strength within ourselves we didn't know we possessed. The crisis becomes a turning point when, perhaps for the first time in our lives, we began to find a spiritual dimension to existence and, having been helped ourselves, we want to do something to help others who are going through the same situation.

This is also true for mediums and healers. Many of those I have spoken to have told me that they began their work following a period in their lives when they were at their lowest ebb because of bereavement, illness or problems of some kind or another. As one of them put it to me, 'How can I be sympathetic to my sitters, and know what they are going through, unless I have been there myself?'

In my case, it was my father's death that led me to seek knowledge of spirit communication and, through that, to develop my own gift of mediumship. Now I no longer mourn him or wish he was back here because I know he is much happier and more fulfilled in his present life and that, no matter what happens to me, he will never be beyond my call.

It may be that you have the ability yourself to be aware of loved ones around you. If you have lost someone you love, and think you can still feel their presence, don't dismiss it as imagination. Most probably they are there, trying to get through to you. Send out a loving thought to them and don't have any fear. Know that they will be aware of your thoughts, even if you cannot see or hear them. Take comfort in the wordless communication that unites those who love across the bridge of death.

A canon of St Paul's Cathedral, Henry Scott-Holland, wrote these words in 1918:

Death is nothing at all ... I have only slipped away into the next room. I am I, and you are you ... whatever we were to each other, that we are still.

Call me by my old familiar name, speak to me in the easy way which you always used. Put no difference into your tone; wear no forced air of solemnity or sorrow.

Laugh as we always laughed at the little jokes we enjoyed together. Play, smile, think of me, pray for me.

Let my name be ever the household word that it always was. Let it be spoken without effect, without the ghost of a shadow on it.

Life means all that it ever meant. It is the same as it ever was; there is absolutely unbroken continuity.

What is this death but a negligible accident? Why should I be out of mind because I am out of sight?

I am but waiting for you, for an interval, somewhere very near, just around the corner ... All is well.

4 Mysteries of the Séance Room

Every now and then a writer has to eat her words, and this is one of those times. In my last book I implied that the traditional séance, held in a darkened room, was a thing of the past. True, such séances are still very rare. No one who visits a church or goes to a medium for a sitting needs to fear that they will find the place blacked out, with phantom forms floating eerily about. But, as I mentioned in my introduction, physical mediumship has not completely died out. In fact, it now seems to be enjoying something of a revival.

Before we go any further, it might be helpful to explain the difference between physical and mental mediumship. The term 'mental mediumship' covers what is usually called clairvoyance, in which the medium receives 'messages' or communications from the world of spirit which she passes on to the sitters. Everything that she sees, hears or senses is conveyed through her mind alone. The sitters do not see or hear anything and have to take the medium's word for whatever comes through. In the case of physical mediumship, however, anyone sitting with the medium can see and hear what is happening. The term covers all types of manifestations, from table rapping and levitation to the production of spirit voices and – most incredible of all – the appearance of materialized spirit forms.

A hundred years ago, physical mediumship was what Spiritualism was all about. Clairvoyance as we know it today was a later development. People would sit round the parlour table calling out the letters of the alphabet again and again, waiting for the table to tilt, turn or rap when the appropriate letter was reached. This was very time consuming and, after the initial fascination wore off, must have been extremely tedious. But gradually the spirit repertoire expanded. According to contemporary accounts, tables, and sometimes the mediums themselves, would levitate. Trumpets – metal cones painted with luminous paint at both ends – flew around the room, through which the spirit voices spoke. Musical instruments played by themselves. Hands appeared that tapered off at the wrists in a cloud of ectoplasm.

Things became even more exciting with the invention of the cabinet. This was either a box like a sentry box or perhaps a curtained off alcove of the room. Its purpose was to build up the power needed for the phenomena to take place. The medium, in trance, sat inside. After a few minutes the curtains would part and spirit faces would appear. On occasion, complete spirit forms, clad in white drapery, might emerge, walk around the room and converse with the sitters.

One of the most famous mediums of the era was Florence Cook. The scientist Sir William Crookes investigated her carefully over a period of months. He claimed that a spirit who called herself Katie King appeared many times, fully materialized. He even took photographs showing her and the medium side by side.

This was too much for the critics, who declared that Crookes was either being deceived or was colluding with the medium in faking the séances. A spirit who was real and solid, yet who could vanish instantly in a puff of smoke – who could believe such preposterous nonsense? It was in vain for the Spiritualists to maintain that manifestations such as this did take place with a number of different mediums. If it really happened, sceptics demanded to know, why couldn't spirits appear in broad daylight, instead of in dark rooms, where the possibilities for fraud were many and obvious?

Spiritualists retaliated that the forms were composed of ectoplasm, a substance drawn from the medium, which could only be produced in darkness because it dissolved in bright light. Unfortunately, they could not give a satisfactory explanation of the nature of this mysterious substance, which bore a suspicious resemblance to cheesecloth or muslin, though those who had seen and handled it claimed that it behaved in a way that no man-made cloth could do. Why were mediums so reluctant for these forms to be touched, sceptics equired? The Spiritualists replied that this was very dangerous for the medium. If she was startled, the ectoplasm would rush back into her body, causing shock or even physical injury. The explanations sounded a little too much like convenient excuses and the cause was not helped by the fact that the photographs taken by Crookes and others looked phoney even if they were genuine. The case was made more difficult to defend by the fact that fraud was rampant. Time after time, mediums were caught blatantly impersonating their spirits. But despite this – and far-fetched though it may seem – there is some very stong evidence from reliable witnesses that astonishing phenomena did occur.

D.D. Home, probably the most amazing medium of all time, was never caught out in any kind of trickery, yet hundreds of people, on different occasions, saw him levitate, saw spirit hands and heard musical instruments play when no one was near them. Crookes records how on one occasion he and his wife saw, in good light, 'a cloudy appearance which seemed to condense into a distinct human form, clothed in flimsy drapery.' The figure took an accordion which Crookes was holding and played it, walking around the room as it did so. As it touched Mrs Crookes, she screamed and the apparition seemed to sink into the floor to the waist, still playing the accordion as it went!

The naturalist Alfred Russel Wallace described a séance with a medium called Monck which took place in the full light of day, during which he saw a faint white patch on the medium's coat which grew brighter and extended until it formed a cloudy pillar extending from his shoulders to his feet. The pillar then assumed the form of a thickly draped woman who, after a brief period of time, appeared to be reabsorbed into the medium's body.

But no amount of testimony like this could make the critics take the Spiritualists' claims seriously. A small band of scientists including Crookes, Wallace and Sir Oliver Lodge, risked their reputations by stating their beliefs but they were ridiculed. The Society for Psychical Research, founded in 1882 by a group of Cambridge academics, looked into the matter and collected some remarkable evidence but the Society, containing a high percentage of sceptics in any case, soon turned its attention to the investigation of mental mediumship.

Among the general public, the craze for phenomena declined and physical mediumship went out of fashion. However, the early years of the twentieth century did produce a few notable physical mediums, and some notable investigators who approached the subject in a scientific way, determined to establish once and for all if there was any truth behind it.

In the 1920s the French physiologist Professor Charles Richet conducted a serious of experiments with a medium called Marthe Bérand (also known as Eva C.). He took stringent precautions against fraud. Before each séance the medium was undressed and searched. Richet was able to witness the whole process of materialization. In *Thirty Years of Psychical Research* he gives a detailed description, which actually sounds rather revolting.

A kind of liquid or pasty jelly emerges from the mouth or the breast of Marthe which organizes itself by degrees, acquiring the shape of a face or a limb. Under very good conditions of visibility, I have seen this paste spread on my knee, and slowly take form so as to show the rudiment of the radius, the cubitus, or metacarpal bone whose increasing pressure I could feel on my knee.

These materializations are usually gradual, beginning by a rudimentary shape, complete forms and human faces only appearing later on. At first these formations are often very imperfect. Sometimes they show no relief, looking more like flat images than bodies, so that in spite of oneself one is inclined to imagine some fraud, since what appears seems to be the materialization of a semblance, and not of a being. But in some cases the materialization is perfect. At the Villa Carmen I saw a fully organized form rise from the floor. At first it was only a white, opaque spot like a handkerchief lying on the ground before the curtain, then this handkerchief quickly assumed the form of a human head level with the floor, and a few moments later it rose up in a straight line and became a small man enveloped in a kind of white burnous, who took two or three halting steps in front of the curtain and then sank to the floor and disappeared as if through a trap-door. But there was no trap-door.

Dr Gustave Geley confirmed Richet's findings. He studied the ectoplasm, noting that it took various forms from sheets to thin threads that were sometimes soft and sometimes hard to the touch. He observed that it was extremely sensitive to light and touch and was constantly in motion, forming shapes and forms that built up and disintegrated under his eyes. All this took place while Marthe was in trance, and while her hands were being held by the sitters on either side of her.

So what was the ectoplasm? Another researcher, Schrenck Notzing, succeeded in capturing some in a test tube and had it analysed. He found that it contained 'conglomerates of bodies resembling epithelium, real plate epithelium with nuclei, veil-like flimsy structures, coherent lamellar bodies without structure, as well as flat globules and mucus.' In other words, it was of organic origin, which doesn't tell us a lot, except that it was definately not cheesecloth. He surmised that it was 'a sort of transitory matter which originates in the organism in a manner unknown to us, possesses unknown biological functions and formative possibilities and is evidently particularly dependent on the psychic influence of the medium.'

The Spiritualists explained it in this way: The spirit body, in which we exist after death, is a replica of the physical body, though composed of finer substance, which is why it is normally invisible to human sight. The ectoplasm which is taken from the medium and always remains connected to her is moulded by the spirit operators around the spirit form, making it solid and visible. If there is not much power, only part of the body may be materialized, a face perhaps or a hand, but when the power is strong the complete form can be built up.

Some startling manifestations were produced by a Polish medium, Franek Kluski. Kluski's speciality was animals. A whole menagerie of them appeared at his séances. Cats and dogs ran around the room and jumped onto the sitters' laps. A lion came that would stalk around, lashing its tail against the furniture and leaving behind it a strong acrid smell. Sometimes an ape-like creature appeared, resembling a primitive man, which allowed its fur to be stroked and scratched the hands of the sitters lightly with its claws. Fortunately, it seems to have been friendly. It was photographed a number of times by researchers who had taken the precaution of searching the medium and the room beforehand – and declared that there was no way in which Kluski could have been faking.

Other well-known physical mediums such as Margery Crandon and Rudi Schneider were the subject of scientific investigation in the twenties and thirties, but they were the last of a dying breed. There was, however, one medium whose name was a household word: Helen Duncan.

Mrs Duncan is still remembered today by many people who had sittings with her, who claim that she had remarkable powers, but her career was dogged with accusations of fraud. In 1944 a séance she was giving was interrupted by the police, who burst in and arrested her. She was brought to trial at the Old Bailey and accused under the antiquated Witchcraft Act of 1735 of 'pretending to conjure up spirits'.

The case caused a sensation. The prosecution alleged that she had been using a white muslin sheet to impersonate the spirit forms. As no trace of this sheet was found, the absurd suggestion was made that she had swallowed it. Defence counsel claimed that the 'sheet' was ectoplasm, which, when she was seized, had rushed back into her body, causing considerable damage to her health.

The trial lasted for seven days. Numerous witnesses spoke in her defence, declaring that, on other occasions, they had seen her produce phenomena that was undoubtedly genuine. Hundreds of other witnesses expressed their willingness to appear. Mrs Duncan herself offered to demonstrate her gifts in front of the court, but this was refused. She was sentenced to six months' imprisonment, most of which, because of her poor state of health, was spent in the prison hospital.

It seems extraordinary that, in the middle of the war, so much time and trouble should have been devoted to what in the eyes of the authorities was an insignificant case, but some people suspected that there was a more sinister motive behind Mrs Duncan's arrest. At one séance, a sailor had materialized who gave his mother details of the ship on which he had been sailing. As news of the sinking of the ship had not then been released to the public, the mother contacted the Admiralty to verify what she had been told. Shortly afterwards, she receive a visit from two Admiralty officials who wanted to know how she had come by the information. Mrs Duncan's arrest took place three weeks later and it was suggested that the trial was concocted in order to prevent her from giving away any more official secrets.

Upon her release, Mrs Duncan resumed her work but once more came under suspicion. In 1956 the police again raided a séance she was giving. Nothing fraudulent was found, but she collapsed and was taken to hospital, where she died a few weeks later, officially of diabetes, but more probably of the shock she received from being disturbed while in trance. Spiritualists regarded her as a martyr for the cause. Her trial did have one positive result. The Witchcraft Act was replaced by the fairer Fraudulent Mediums Act, which is still in force.

I have spoken to a number of people who remember Helen Duncan and all of them spoke highly of her and vouched for her honesty. One person who has fond memories of her is Alan Crossley, who sat with her many times during his forty years of psychical research. He explained that her guide, Albert, would always appear first and the sitters could see the two figures distinctly; Mrs Duncan, short and stout, sitting in the chair and Albert, who was over six feet tall, standing beside her. Alan's book *The Enigma of Psychic Phenomenon* describes a typical séance:

As soon as the introduction was over the 'guide' escorted his medium back to her chair and, with a swish, pulled the curtains together. The audience sang the Lord's Prayer softly until 'Albert' again addressed the audience. 'The first person to come here from our side of life is a gentleman who passed as a result of a heart condition. He has only been here for a short while ... he is coming for someone sitting next to you Alan.' There was a slight pause, and, continuing 'Albert' said, 'Will that lady sitting next to Alan ask a gentleman out?' Sitting next to me was a friend and her son, whom I had persuaded to attend in the hope that her husband would manifest. He had died in hospital only a few days previously, following an operation for a stomach ulcer. The medical staff, however, failed to observe that he had an abscess close to the heart! This burst, and resulted in his death. This gentleman was my former boss and I knew him very well. Slowly, the curtains parted revealing a figure smiling broadly. I recognised him immediately! Looking directly toward his wife he gasped excitedly, 'Hello, darling.' His son jumped up from his seat and shouted 'Skipper!' He had recognised his father. The moment was dramatic and electrifying. His wife tried to speak but was so overcome with emotion that she found it impossible. 'My dearest,' said her husband, 'I want you to carry on from where I left off.' Then, with a wink in my direction, he said, 'Thank you, Alan, for your help in making this possible.' He moved back a little, threw a kiss to his wife and son, and then dematerialised, seemingly through the floor!

Among the many other materialisations that evening, I must mention the mother who had lost her twin babies soon after they were born. Both materialised in the arms of Mrs Duncan, screaming their heads off! The mother went up to the cabinet and took a close look at them. From her reaction there was little doubt that they belonged to her.

One of the most moving stories about Helen Duncan was given to me by Georgina Brake, whose husband of five weeks, Ronald, was drowned during the Second World War. A couple of years later, she decided to marry a young man who had been a mutual friend of her and Ronald but she wanted to be sure that Ronald approved of their marriage.

Two weeks before the wedding, she and her fiancé Bob were invited to attend a séance with Helen Duncan. Before the proceedings began, Mrs Duncan was taken into another room by two of the sitters, where she changed into black clothes.

The séance was held in an ordinary sitting room, in a very dignified manner with an opening prayer followed by hymns, used to raise the vibrations, there being no tape recorders in those days. Two black curtains were draped across the corner of the room forming a cabinet, in which Helen Duncan sat. In a little while her breathing became heavy and then we heard a voice saying, 'Good evening everybody! It gives me great pleasure to be with you again this evening. For those of you who have not sat with us before, I will show you that through which I am speaking.' The curtains parted and out floated a mike, not like those used today but a square box like arrangement made of ectoplasm, on a rod that came up out of the floor.

'I am the guide, the operator behind the scenes. My name is Albert.' The voice was clear and had a metallic sound just as if being spoken through a microphone.

'I will now show myself to you.' A hand came round the curtain, pulling it back and there stood a tall man with a dark beard, very distinguished looking, draped from head to foot in white ectoplasm, which looked like the fine white net. Albert explained that there were many friends waiting to speak to us, and would we please welcome them. There then appeared the materialised forms, I should think about ten.

Albert then said, 'I've an elderly lady here who died when she was 72. She says she was very crippled with arthritis, and she wishes to speak to her granddaughter.' Before anything more could be said, out stepped my dear old Granny, my father's mother, who I loved dearly. She was only about 5 ft tall and there she stood, all draped in ectoplasm and this is what she said;

'Hello Ena, hello Bob. You don't know me Bob, but I know you. You just look after my girl!'

I said, 'Is it really you Granny?'

'Do you want me to prove it?' she said, and with that she turned sideways and screwed up her face and said, 'Don't I look like Punch?' This she did when I was a little girl to make me laugh. Granny had a full set of dentures, but they were always in a glass by the side of her bed except when she went out. The absence of teeth had caused her mouth to recede, and if she screwed up her face her chin and nose almost met, making her look like Punch, of Punch and Judy. No one could possibly have known this, it was absolute proof that it was Granny. With that she said 'Goodbye, give my love to Connie and George and tell them that there's no more pain.' Connie and George were my mother and father.

Albert then said, 'I have a young man here who lost his life at sea, and he tells me that his body has never been brought out of the water. He has come to speak to his wife.'

Bob encouraged me to speak, and I said, 'Come on dear, come and speak to me.' The curtains parted and out stepped dear Ron, who said, 'Hello darling, I've come to give you my blessing. I want you to know that your happiness is my happiness always. Take care of her Bob until she can join me, and thank you both for what you've had done with my ring.'

When Ronald and I married, at my request he bought me a gold cross and chain. My wedding ring was very precious to me and Bob paid to have it joined to the cross, making a cross within a circle, a sacred symbol. It was round my neck under my blouse during the séance, where it is today, and has been during the last 50 years. Only my family and close friends know of its existence.

A medium who was never as well-known as Helen Duncan but who had remarkable gifts, was Alec Harris. Alan Crossley witnessed some very strange happenings with him.

The medium entered the séance room wearing only a black track suit and sat in the corner of the room between two black curtains. A dim red light was situated just above him and he was clearly visible. Within a matter of seconds from the commencement of the séance, a figure materialised and walked toward the centre of the circle. This figure was followed by another and then a third figure emerged. The first was that of a North American Indian, sporting a magnificent headdress with feathers extending to the floor. The second was a small Chinese gentleman dressed in rich silk robes, a black hat and a pigtail which hung from the back and across one of his shoulders. The third was an Egyptian who remained close to the medium. The other two figures walked slowly round the circle so that we could observe them closely. During this time, the medium was still in his chair, head leaning to one side and obviously in a deep trance. From an occasional snore and grunt, one might easily have thought that he was simply asleep. Then something happened which I believed was hardly credible, in fact impossible. The medium was sitting in his chair, but minus his head! The following seconds revealed that he was in the process of dematerialisation! I saw him gradually disappear until only the chair remained. Crazy? In fact impossible, but it happened. I looked round the circle to see the reaction of the other sitters and wondered if they had noticed this extraordinary incident. Unable to resist any longer, I queried what I believed had happened, just in case it could have been an hallucination! An immediate response came from the medium's wife. 'Oh, it's alright,' she said. 'He will be some where around, they often take him away.' At this, the North American Indian assured everyone that the medium was alright and would return shortly. However, later on the Indian turned to the medium's wife and said, 'I want you to unlock the door, go downstairs and into the garden. There you will find your husband on his knees. Wake him up and bring him back to the séance room!' She promptly obeyed the instruction and returned with Alec who calmly took his seat and slipped into trance again. The three materialisations had, through all this, remained and held conversations with the sitters!

Jack Webber, who died in 1940, is also well remembered today. Like Alec Harris, he came from Wales but during the course of his short career he travelled all over Britain demonstrating his mediumship before thousands of people in small home circles and public halls. Webber never sat in a cabinet, fearing that this might give rise to accusations of fraud. He always insisted on being roped to his chair, inviting the sitters to tie him up in any way they liked and to inspect the ropes again at the end of the proceedings to ensure that they had not been tampered with in any way. In addition to these precautions, he encouraged the use of infra-red cameras so that any phenomena that took place could be recorded. These photographs show the ectoplasm issuing from his mouth, nose and ears and unwinding itself down the front of his body to the floor. Rods of ectoplasm were also captured on camera, holding trumpets, which flew around the room at great speed and were often still in motion when the guide called for the lights to be put on. Voices were heard speaking through them, sometimes more than one at once, coming from different parts of the room. Although he was an uneducated man, these voices spoke to the sitters in their own languages. One of the guides who called himself Reuben had such a fine singing voice that Decca made a record of him singing hymns.

But the most remarkable feature of Webber's mediumship, and the one for which he was most famous, was the removal by supernatural means of his coat. This was witnessed on many occasions, the coat being apparently dematerialized and materialized again, without disturbing the ropes with which the medium was bound.

The journalist Cassandra, who claimed that he could bring as much scepticism to bear on Spiritualism as any writer living, attended one of the séances and was impressed in spite of himself. He saw a heavy table levitate, saw trumpets shoot around the room 'like a fish in a tank,' heard a voice speak and felt himself being splashed with water, though there was no water in the room. He admitted, 'I went there to scoff, but the laugh is sliding slowly round to the other side of my face.'

Ruth Atkins, who is now in her eighties, gave me her account of a Webber séance she attended at a small private sanctuary in Wimbledon.

There were about fifteen of us there. It was evening but the room was not dark; there was sufficient light for us to see each other clearly. Jack sat by the large bay window. He had a trolley beside him on which there were various toys; a ball, a toy train and a ball. We all sat round in a circle on wooden armchairs. There was an infra-red lamp in the corner of the room.

Before we started, Jack asked one of the sitters, a Mr Evett who was a tailor, to sew him into his waistcoat. Mr Evett sewed him in securely with cross-stitches and my husband tied his wrists and ankles to the chair. We joined hands and sat for a while, talking in ordinary voices. Then the bell on the trolley rose up into the air and rang. The toy train rose up next and travelled round the whole circle and went back onto the trolley again. The ball fell onto the floor. No one moved. I saw the ectoplasm form into a blue light over Mrs Evett's head then a face appeared in it in miniature. Mrs Evett saw it too. It was her mother.

Towards the end of the séance we all saw his waistcoat lifted over his head and thrown onto the floor. It landed at Mr Evett's feet. It was still sewn up just as it had been before – the stitches hadn't been touched. And the medium was still wearing his jacket.

Then the most amazing thing happened. The whole chair, with the medium on it, was lifted up into the air and came to rest in front of my husband. The knots were tied and he and Mr Evett had secured them and had not been disturbed. Gradually, Jack came round. We kept him quiet for a while. He needed time to recover. The work took a lot out of him. He gave himself so freely to the spirit power. He treated it as though it was a perfectly normal thing. It was overwhelming. You couldn't be frightened and you couldn't have any doubts about it.

Tom Harrison had many years in which to study physical phenomena. His mother, Minnie Harrison, was a remarkable medium. From 1946 into the mid fifites she gave regular séances in her home which were attended by her family and friends and sometimes by visitors. An amateur photographer, Tom took many photographs, one of which is produced here (Plate 5). It shows ectoplasm, in the shape of a rod, being used to control a trumpet.

Photographs like these lend credulity to what would otherwise be an almost unbelievable phenomenon. Actually, I am aware that I may already have strained some reader's credulity too far. Even people who have related to me their experiences of the séance room have often prefaced their accounts, somewhat apologetically, by remarks like, 'I don't suppose you're going to believe me, but ...' Nevertheless, strange things do happen and it is as well to keep an open mind.

I have only once taken part in a séance where physical phenomena occurred, which, considering that I have been involved in Spiritualism for twenty years, shows how rare it is.

The séance took place at the Wimbledon home of a medium called Owen Potts. There were about six other sitters present. Most of them were known to me. We sat in a circle in Owen's sitting-room. The room was dark but there was just enough light to make out the outlines of the other sitters. While Owen was going quietly into trance, we were asked to sing; the sound of voices is supposed to 'raise the vibrations'. With more enthusiasm than tunefulness, we lauched into a rousing chorus of some popular song.

After a few minutes, Owen's guide came through and delivered some messages, the contents of which I have forgotten. Then we were told that Jim, the deceased brother of one of the sitters, had a present for each of us. The trumpet rose up into the air and whizzed round very fast above our heads. It paused just over my head then tipped downwards. I felt a soft plop as something dropped into my lap. When the lights were put on, I saw what it was; a tightly closed pink rosebud. Each sitter had received a similar gift.

This was not a séance held under strict conditions. It was simply a circle of friends sitting together. I admit that it would have been possible for someone present to have moved the trumpet although it would have been difficult, in such a confined space, to wave it round so fast without falling over someone's feet. The flowers could theoretically have been concealed in the room beforehand but I am convinced that no such trickery was involved, since the medium was someone I knew and respected and the other sitters were experienced and not the type of people to be easily taken in. It sounds incredible but it happened – and the sequel was even more curious.

One of the sitters had brought with him a new tape, which he set up in his recorder at the beginning of the session. As we sat having a cup of tea afterwards, we played it back. We would not have been surprised if the recording was blank. Psychic energy can have strange effects on electrical equipment, as Uri Geller and numerous other psychics have demonstrated. But what we heard left us all speechless.

The medium's and the sitters' voice could be heard quite clearly but in the background was a cacophony of noises that had nothing to do with us. There were mumbled voices, too indistinct to make out the words and there was singing, some of it dignified, like church music but some raucous, as though we had accidentally tuned into a knees-up in the astral equivalent of the Rose and Crown.

Our first thought was that the tape had picked up sounds from a radio or television in an adjacent house but the sounds were too disorganized for that. Sometimes the noise was so loud that it drowned out the sounds of our own voices, and had it come from any natural source, we would certainly have heard it ourselves while the séance was going on. We were quite at a loss to account for it.

But that was not all. One of the sitters took the tape home and re-recorded it to play to a friend who was interested in psychical research and knew something about recording equipment, hoping he would be able to offer some explanation. Yet when she played back the second recording she found that the background noises had completely disappeared. It is a mystery that still baffles me.

Recently, I spoke to Owen, who has now given up physical mediumship in order to concentrate on his work as a hypnotherapist. I asked him what sensations he felt during the séances. He told me that he remembered very little about it, since most of the time he was in deep trance.

'My method was to put myself into trance by self-hypnosis. I would close my eyes and see a light in the distance. The light would grow bigger and brighter until I became absorbed into it. After that, I knew nothing more until I came to when the séance ended.'

Owen's regular sitters included Lee Everett, wife of Kenny Everett, and a medium herself. They experienced some remarkable phenomena, which included the production of apports, objects transported into the séance by supernatural means. On one occasion, one of their spirit visitors, obviously a character with a sense of humour, asked if they would like a drink. Naturally, they replied that they would. When the lights were put on, there in the middle of the circle was a tray of wine glasses complete with wine, apported apparently from some unsuspecting person's party, though Owen never did discover exactly where they had come from.

The levitation of trumpets, such as I witnessed, was a regular occurence. Voices spoke through them, sometimes deceased friends of relations of the sitters, sometimes guides who gave philosophical teachings. Owen explained that the power to produce the phenomena was produced not only from him as the medium and from the other sitters, but was also drawn from objects in the room. Even water could be used for this purpose. Sometimes they would find at the end of a séance that the water in the vases of flowers had been drained dry.

I asked Owen whether he had felt any adverse effects from this work, and whether it placed a strain on the medium's health. He agreed that this was a danger and pointed out that many physical mediums suffer from heart trouble and other disabilities. Jack Webber, for instance, died at the age of thirty-three and Helen Duncan suffered from a variety of health problems, including diabetes, which may have been caused or aggravated by the work she did. Owen himself had a heart attack, possibly as a result of the séances, which drained so much of his mental and physical energy.

With such risks involved, it is not surprising that very few mediums are willing to undertake this type of work. When, a few years ago, I enquired of the Spiritualists National Union how many physical mediums there were in the country today I was told that there was only one who was giving public demonstrations, and that was the Union's president, Gordon Higginson. He, like Owen, has now given up physical séances for health reasons.

However, as I said earlier, physical mediumship has suddenly and unexpectedly started enjoying a revival. This is due, at least in part, to the efforts of an organization of which Alan Crossley is the president. The Noah's Ark Society exists to promote the safe development and practise of physical mediumship. It takes its name and its inspiration from the medium Noah Zerdin, who died in 1972. Although it was only formed in 1990, membership has grown rapidly and it now has over 400 members, many of whom are sitting in their own development circles. According to the chairman, Robin Foy, they are getting very encouraging results.

I have to say that, when I first heard of the society, I had my doubts about it. Weren't they trying to put the clock back, to revive a form of mediumship that belonged to the past?

This is an objection that Robin has encountered many times. He answers it by saying that physical mediumship has its place, not to replace the kind of mediumship we are familiar with, but to exist alongside it.

'With clairvoyance,' he explained to me, 'however good it is, there is always an element of doubt, but you can't doubt what you can see and hear for yourself.'

He is aware that not everyone within the Spiritualist movement agrees with what the society is trying to do.

'A lot of people are doubtful about this kind of phenomena. They feel that it's been discredited by the fraud that went on – even though there were some fine genuine mediums.'

But he believes that things are different now. Modern technology can be used in investigations. The society has purchased a number of special cameras that are able to film in total darkness. These can be set up just a few feet away from the medium and the results can be recorded directly onto a video recorder. This is obviously of great benefit to researchers, but it is also of benefit to the mediums.

'In the past mediums were subjected to all sorts of indignities. They were stripped, searched, tied up and put in boxes, to make sure they didn't move while the séance was in progress and fake the effects. Sometimes, like Helen Duncan, they suffered actual physical injury when a suspicious sitter put the lights on or grabbed hold of one of the materialized forms. None of this need happen today. It would be impossible for a medium to cheat with the camera so close.'

Robin believes that, as technology has moved on in our world, so scientists in the next world have also been experimenting and refining their techniques, so that phenomena can be produced by methods that are not as harmful or as tiring to the medium. One sign of this change is the way in which the process of development has speeded up.

'In the past, mediums would sometimes sit in circles for years before they got results. Now we are finding, in the circles associated with the society, that things often start to happen within a few months.'

He emphasizes that most of the circles are still in the early stages, but already some of them are experiencing the levitation of tables, the movement of trumpets and 'independent voice' – spirit voices that speak out of mid-air.

These results can only come, however, if someone within the circle has the potential for physical mediumship. There is some debate as to whether, in general terms, mediums have to be born with their gifts or whether the ability can be developed. As far as physical mediumship is concerned, Robin has no doubt.

'A physical medium has to have something in their bodily make-up which makes it possible for them to produce ectoplasm. The gift is extremely rare – perhaps only one person in several thousand has that quality.'

As with all types of mediumship, where the potential exists it usually shows itself in the form of some sort of phenomena – unexplained noises, for instance or perhaps poltergeist activity –

which take place in the person's vicinity and which, if they don't understand what is happening, can be very frightening. Robin himself is quite used to this as he and his wife have a lot of paranormal activity within their home. It is not unusual for them to find objects moved or the radiators turned on or off but they accept this quite calmly as signs of spirit friends around them.

Anyone who seriously wants to develop this form of mediumship has to have great dedication. It is definitely not for sensation-seekers, nor is it for those of a nervous disposition. No one who is afraid of sitting in the dark, or who is likely to run out of the room screaming if the table moves, should sit in a physical circle. As with all mediumship, anyone who is mentally unbalanced should leave it well alone. Commonsense is an essential requirement.

A great deal of patience is required; patience to continue sitting, regularly and faithfully, even when nothing seems to be happening. Robin advises circles to give it a few months before expecting results. If, at the end of this time, there is still not so much as a rap on the table, it might be time to consider whether it's worth pursuing the attempts any further. It may be that the conditions are not right, or that no one within the group has the requisite power. The society will visit circles, if requested, to give help and advice. Even when things are going well, there are likely to be some blank sittings, especially in the early stages and success can never be guaranteed.

However, the members of the society are very enthusiastic and are determined to ensure that physical phenomena once more take their place as a recognized and very exciting form of mediumship. Robin sees the society as a safe haven in which mediums can develop their gifts safely and under controlled conditions. Then, when they are sufficiently prepared, members of the public and scientists can be invited in to witness the séances. Eventually, he hopes that materialized forms, which can be seen and touched, will be able to appear in lighted rooms, while the whole proceedings are recorded on video.

'If we can achieve this,' he says, 'it will be the ultimate proof of survival. No one will be able to doubt the evidence.'

5 Voices on the Medium Wave

The recording we made at that séance was certainly extraordinary but the voices of the dead have been captured many times on tape. Electronic voice phenomena first became well-known with the publication in 1971 of *Breakthrough* by Konstantin Raudive. Since then a considerable amount of research has been done into this new means of communicating with the other side.

The technique is not as simple as you might suppose. You can do as we did, merely put a blank tape into the machine, let it record then play it back, but, for reasons to be explained later, this doesn't usually work. There is evidence to suggest that the presence of people with mediumistic ability may aid the recording, which is perhaps why we were so successful, but the method most commonly used is to link the tape-recorder to the radio, using the white noise between stations as a background. This, of course, means that the tape will pick up a variety of stray signals, resulting in a confusion of sound. So how can you be sure that the voices are really there?

The best way is to hear them for yourself and in order to do that, I went to visit one of the country's leading experts on EVP, George Gilbert Bonner. Gilbert has been studying EVP since 1972. Like many researchers in this field, he was initially inspired by reading *Breakthrough*. Being trained in psychology, his first reaction to the book was that the author was either self-deluded or else deceiving his readers but, following the instructions given, he took his reel to reel tape-recorder and battery radio, set it up and, feeling very foolish, spoke into the microphone. 'Can anyone hear me? Would anyone like to speak to me?'

He heard nothing until he rewound the tape and played it again. Then he heard his own voice, followed by a hiss and a rush of sound – and then a voice that sounded like someone calling down a long tunnel replied with a long drawn out, 'Yes!'

'It was an eerie feeling,' Gilbert admitted, but he considers that he was fortunate to get results so quickly; some tapers have to make recordings and play them back for months before getting a response.

Since then he has recorded over 50,000 voices but he accepts as definitely paranormal only those which call his name, comment on something he has said or make remarks that are comprehensible and relevant.

Gilbert took me into his laboratory, filled with recording equipment and stacks of tapes, and sat me down in front of the tape-recorder.

'You might not hear anything at first,' he warned. 'It takes practice to pick out the voices.'

I listened through the headphones. As he had anticipated, all I could hear was noise of the kind you get when the radio is between stations, not tuned in properly. He played the relevant part of the tape several times. Suddenly I heard it – the faint but unmistakable sound of a man's voice saying, 'Calling Gilbert Bonner ... calling Gilbert Bonner!'

It was a thrilling moment. As a medium I am used to hearing voices speak to me inside my head, but hearing a spirit voice on a tape – it brought the spirit world strangely closer. And it was, as he said, an eerie feeling.

Gilbert played me some more tapes. I found that, with practice, the voices were easier to make out. Rather like riding a bicycle, there's a knack to it and once you've mastered it, you wonder why you found it so difficult before. The voices spoke in short phrases as if they were making an effort to speak, and short bursts of sound were all they could produce. They varied in quality. Tapers classify voices as A, B and C according to their clarity. Many of Gilbert's are of the A type, clear enough to be heard by anyone and with no doubt about what they are saying. His own name is mentioned many times, as is that of Raudive. Phrases such as 'friends are gathered' and 'Bonner, we are talking' occur frequently. As a method of communication it is obviously extremely limited but the voices are there and cannot be explained away.

The idea of recording the voices of the dead is as old as the use of recording equipment. In the 1920s the American scientist

Thomas Edison, who invented the phonograph, tried to devise an instrument capable of communicating with the dead. He surmised that, if the personality survives death, those in the world beyond should be able to affect physical matter, if only equipment could be devised sensitive enough for them to manipulate. Most people at the time thought that he had taken leave of his senses and in fact Edison was unsuccessful in his experiments. However, forty years later he was vindicated by the Swede, Friedrich Jürgenson.

Jürgenson was a man of many talents; artist, opera singer and documentary film producer. One day, when recording bird song for a film he was making, he took his battery operated tape recorder into a wood near his home in Stockholm and set it up. When he played the recording back he was astonished to hear on the tape, as well as the noise of chirping, the faint sound of human voices talking about the habits of birds.

His first thought was that he had picked up a stray radio transmission but a month later he heard other voices on tapes, some of which addressed him by name. Among them was one saying, 'Friedal, my little Friedal, can you hear me?' With a shock, he recognized it as the voice of his mother, who had died four years before.

Jürgenson became convinced that he had been chosen to receive the voices of the dead. He continued recording, experimenting with different techniques, until he had collected hundreds of voices on tape.

He wrote a book, *Voices of the Universe*, which attracted great public interest. It also attracted the attention of the German parapsychologist Professor Dr Hans Bender, who set up a team of scientists to study the phenomenon.

Bender concluded that the voices were of paranormal origin but refused to concede that they came from the dead. He surmised that some kind of psychokinetic energy was involved, that in some way the operator impressed his thoughts onto the tape. This theory, or variations of it, has frequently been put forward by other parapsychologists since then.

However, Jürgenson did apparently find a sympathetic ear in the Vatican. The Catholic church has never expressed any official interest in the voices but a number of distinguished Catholic priests and scientists have conducted research of their own, and in 1969 Pope Paul VI decorated Jürgenson with the

Commander's Cross of the Order of St Gregory the Great.

Jürgenson's work was taken up by Konstantin Raudive, the Latvian psychologist and philosopher. Raudive was so fascinated by Jürgenson's experiments that he travelled from Germany, where he was then living, to Sweden to meet him. Though initially sceptical, Raudive soon became as convinced as Jürgenson that the voices emanated from the world beyond and on his return to Germany he set up his own experiments, which he continued for many years. By the time of his death in 1974 he had recorded over 72,000 paranormal voices which he claimed gave direct evidence of life after death.

However, the evidence was not as clear-cut as Raudive liked to believe. The voices were extremely difficult to pick out from the background noise of the radio. They spoke in short, staccato phrases at twice the speed of normal speech and in a peculiar sing-song rhythm. They used a mixture of languages, mainly Latvian but with some Russian, German and other European languages thrown in. Frequently more than one language would be used in one phrase or sentence and there were many 'neologisms' or made-up words. Also, a lot of what they said didn't make much sense.

The inference was obvious and the critics were not slow to point it out. Raudive, they suggested, was picking up stray radio transmissions and using his extensive knowledge of languages to interpret the random sounds as voices. There was undoubtedly some truth in this. Other people listening to the recordings heard nothing at all, or else interpreted what the voices were saying in a different way. In one amusing instance, words which Raudive interpreted as a message in Latvian from a deceased friend were identified as the distorted voice of the disc jockey Kid Jensen, announcing a programme on Radio Luxembourg! Unfortunately, Raudive was very dogmatic in his views. He did not take kindly to his interpretations being challenged and showed contempt for anyone who did not agree with his theories, so relations between him and other researchers were frequently strained. There were, however, some remarkably clear voices on the tapes that addressed him by name and alluded to things that were going on in the room while the recordings were being made.

Raudive's book *The Inaudible Made Audible* was brought to the attention of a British publisher, Colin Smythe. Colin Smythe's associate, Peter Bander, was given the task of translating and editing the book but he was far from convinced that the voices were genuine, until a remarkable incident caused him to change his mind.

Unknown to Bander, Colin Smythe had purchased some tapes and made a number of experiments, following the instructions in Raudive's book. He mentioned to Bander that at one particular point on one of the tapes he thought he had detected a voice but he was unable to make out the words. Bander rewound the tape and listened several times to the part in question. At first he heard nothing but noise then, as he was about to give up, his ears picked up the sound of a woman's voice saying in German, 'Why don't you open the door?'

Bander appreciated the relevance of that remark. His office colleagues often reproached him with being unsociable because of his habit of keeping his office door closed. But what impressed him still more was that he instantly recognized the voice as that of his German mother, with whom he had corresponded by tape for several years before her death.

On the basis of this, Bander decided to go ahead with the publication of the book and he invited Raudive to London to demonstrate his tapes in front of journalist and recording engineers. The experiments were supervised by two experts from Pye Records Ltd. Among those present was the chairman of Colin Smythe, Sir Robert Mayer.

Precautions were taken by the engineers to eliminate the possibility of the equipment picking up freak radio emissions of any kind. Nevertheless, when the tape was played back over two hundred voices were discernible on it, some of them so clear that, when they were replayed over the loudspeakers, everyone present could hear them. The engineers were baffled as to how any sound signals could have got past their screening devices.

Among the voices were those of two friends of Mayer's who had recently died, Sir John Barbirolli and the concert pianist Artur Schnabel. Sir Robert's reaction was one of shock. He admitted that, after ninety-two years, it looked as if he would have to adjust himself to the idea of some sort of activity after he had left the earth and he speculated that he might find himself organizing children's concerts in the beyond! His reaction to Bander was enthusiastic.

'Peter, we publish! If the chief engineers of Pye are baffled, I don't see any reason why we should not present this remarkable discovery to the general public.'

The publication of *Breakthrough* heralded the start of a worldwide interest in EVP. Societies were formed in America, Germany and several other European and Scandinavian countries to study the voices and experiments were made using more sophisticated equipment and techniques.

Some researchers claimed to be getting remarkable results. In 1982 George Meek of the Metascience Foundation of North Carolina announced that he and his associate William O'Neill had developed a device which they called the Spiricom with which they could hold two way conversations with the dead. The chief communicator was said to be a Dr Mueller who had died fifteen years before. Meek published details of the construction of the Spiricom but no one else was ever able to replicate O'Neill's results, a fact which threw doubt on the authenticity of the experiments.

In Germany in 1987 the newspaper *Das Neue Blatt* reported how spirit voices had helped to bring a killer to justice. A retired couple who lived in Vienna, George and Hedwig Riedal, had been brutally murdered and the bodies concealed in their flat. There was no obvious suspect but one of their neighbours, Hans Luksch, who had been experimenting for some time with EVP, decided to see if he could contact them on his tape recorder and ask them the identity of the murderer. He gathered a group of friends together and they set up the recording apparatus and called upon the deceased couple to speak. After much crackling and distortion the voice of Hedwig Riedal came through saying a name, Bozidar Sajn.

Luksch told the police who, predictably, laughed at his discovery. Nevertheless, they followed up the lead and traced Sajn, who finally confessed that he had killed the couple because, he said, they annoyed him and he had lost his temper. He was sentenced to life imprisonment.

Meanwhile, in Luxembourg, Jules and Maggie Harsch-Fischbach had begun their experiments. The initial interest came from Maggie. Jules, like many people, was sceptical. When they received the name of Raudive, he asked for proof that it really was him. In answer, he was given a telephone number in Germany. He rang the number, and found himself speaking to a woman who for many years had worked as Raudive's secretary.

After a year and a half of experimenting, the quality of the Fischbachs' recordings suddenly improved dramatically. Now they claim that they receive loud, clear voices with whom they can hold long, sustained conversations and they are given discourses of a philosophical matter as well as technical advice on EVP.

The Fischbachs state that they are in contact with a group of highly evolved personalities who take the collective name of Life-Stream. Among them is an entity who calls himself Technician and says that he is a superhuman being assigned to Planet Earth, but that he never lived on earth in human form. A British EVP expert, Tina Laurent, who visited the Fischbachs, told me that Technician's voice sounded like that of a computer synthesizer. He will apparently speak to any visitors in their own language. During Tina's visit, he told her something that was not known to anyone in the room apart from herself. She was greatly impressed by his dignity and wisdom, so much so that she remarked to her husband on the plane going home, 'I feel as if we have been speaking to God.'

The Fischbachs and some other tapers believe that, just as we have transmitting stations on earth, so there are transmitting stations in the beyond. Both Raudive and Jürgenson believed that there was a sort of central transmitting agency in the next dimension, with teachers to instruct those who wished to speak. This does have a certain logic. No kind of communication between the two worlds is easy and it would make sense that, if we have scientists and technicians here who are seeking to find better methods of communication, their efforts are reciprocated by those on the other side.

Even more curious, some tapers claim to be in contact with extra-terrestrials. Far-fetched though this may sound, it is perhaps significant that the American space agency NASA appears to take an interest in EVP; it is said that the early NASA space flights were bugged by voices speaking in an unknown language and Raudive was visited more than once by engineers from NASA who questioned him closely on his work. Some years ago, Gilbert Bonner was also approached by the electronics division of a major US air base and asked for samples of his recordings, for reasons that were never made clear to him.

Today there are thousands of tapers all over the world although there are only a few in this country where, despite the publication of *Breakthrough*, the subject has never gained wide popularity. The American Association – Electronic Voice Phenomena was founded in 1982 by Sarah Estep. Sarah has written a book, *Voices of Eternity*, in which she describes her experiences. She began recording on the simplest equipment – an old tape-recorder that didn't work properly – and resolved to test the validity of the voices by recording for four hours a day for a week after which, if she had achieved no results, she was going to give up. Nothing happened until the sixth day when, feeling throughly discouraged, she asked a question into the microphone; 'What is your world like?' When she played back the tape she heard in answer a single word – 'Beauty!' Contact had been made.

Some time later, she heard the unmistakable voice of an aunt of whom she had been very fond, and who had died of cancer. The voice spoke with the hoarseness which had been characteristic of her aunt when on earth. Since then Sarah has recorded thousands of voices, in her own home and in other places. She has even made recordings in the pyramids of Egypt, where her tape picked up the sound of beautiful singing in an unknown language. All her voices speak, like Raudive's, in short phrases but they have given verifiable information, described life in the next world and on occasion correctly predicted future events.

Sarah finds her greatest satisfaction in working with those who have been bereaved. On one occasion, she arranged a demonstration for a woman who hoped to make contact with her mother. On playback there was one short phrase, 'I'm busy.' The woman was thrilled. She told Sarah that, since her mother had died five years earlier, she had had three vivid dreams about her, and in each one her mother had told her, 'I'm happy. I'm busy.' This story demonstrates how, in all types of mediumship, the short and apparently trivial message can be of great significance to the person for whom it is intended.

As Sarah says in her book, she feels that she is building a bridge. 'As the one left behind tells the individual that he or she is missed and still loved, and the voice from the next dimension replies, 'I love you, too,' one would have to be devoid of all compassion not to find the moment extremely moving.'

Tina Laurent, whom I mentioned earlier, lives in Wales and studied under the well known parapsychologist Benson Herbert.

She has appeared many times on television and radio and took part in a film made for the American Broadcasting Company by Ronald Reagan's son, Ron Reagan Junior.

Tina often records in places that are reputed to be haunted, simply by holding up the microphone attached to her tape recorder and playing back the tapes and in this way she has captured some uncanny sounds. At a pub in Dyfed where several people have reported supernatural experiences she picked up a voice that seemed to be saying 'Murder!' On some of her visits to haunted sites she was accompanied by the reporter Jenny Longhurst. They visited the church of Ewenny Priory in South Wales, where Tina found the atmosphere sinister enough to make her hair stand on end. The tape caught a voice saying, 'Oh Christine!' and the sound of organ music – even though no one was playing the organ when they were there. The mediaeval walls of Caerphilly Castle contained a ghost with a sense of humour. At one point they were startled by a bat that flew out over their heads. 'Oh, a bat!' Tina exclaimed. When they played back the tape a spectral voice retaliated, 'Bats to you!'

On a few occasions, Tina has recorded names which she had been able to verify. A few months after returning to Wales, having lived for several years in America, she found one day on her tape a voice saying 'Nancy Redwood.' Looking in the phone book, she discovered that there were several Redwoods listed and began ringing them up, starting with those who lived closest to her. On the eighth call an elderly man answered who told her that Nancy Redwood had been his mother's name.

Taking a deep breath, and rather apprehensive of his reaction, Tina asked, 'Would it surprise you to know that she is trying to contact you?'

'Not in the least,' the man replied. 'She was a Spiritualist!'

Tina went to visit him and played the tape to him and his family. She then asked Nancy Redwood to communicate again and give more information about herself. In reply she received one word which she took to be a place name and checked it with Nancy's son.

He admitted that it was close. 'If you change one syllable, that's the name of the place where she used to live.'

All of this indicates the reality of the voices – but how do they get onto the tape? There are various ideas about this and I am indebted to Tina for the following summary of current theories.

The electromagnetic hypothesis: This is the 'radio in the sky' concept which supposes that the voices arrive in the form of ordinary radio signals. (Voices are occasionally heard going onto tape.)

The acoustic hypothesis: This is the 'spirits whisper into the microphone' theory. Under this concept the voices arrive in the form of sound waves, created by vocal cords which are both invisible and immaterial. Presumably, they are at a subaudible level when picked up by the microphone and become audible only after being amplified by the circuits of the recorder.

The combination hypothesis: Here, the entities use more than one means of causing their voices to appear, depending upon the receiving system in use.

The psychokinetic hypothesis: This hypothesis states that an electronic signal, generated by static, broadcast voices or music, background sound, internal white noise etc., exists in all EVP receiving systems, and that at one or more places in the system, this electronic signal is voice-modulated by psychokinetic energy.

Regarding the last hypothesis, it is an interesting fact that EVP sounds are captured on the tape recorded on an individual taper and not on the recorders of others present standing next to them. In other words, it seems that the voices originate in some way within the mechanism of the recorder.

Gilbert Bonner supports the idea that some sort of psychokinetic energy is used. He believes that the communicators either use the free energy produced by the radio transmitters or, more probably, manipulate the existing sound in order to produce voices. This is the reason why it is seldom enough to set up a blank tape in an empty room and let it run although, as we have seen, this can be successful. Generally, however, some sound source needs to be provided and the radio, perhaps because of its electronic nature, seems to be the best such source. Most tapers tune to the 'white noise' or to radio 'mush', the random noise heard when the radio is tuned between stations. Other sound sources can be used such as running water or even the drone of traffic outside, and these sounds too may be modulated to resemble voices.

Curious anomalies sometimes occur, indicating that the electrical equipment is being used in ways we don't understand.

For instance, simultaneously run tapes can give different results. Sounds such as music, whistles, scratches or bangs may be heard as well as voices. Voices are sometimes found on the reverse side of tapes. They appear when the tape is twisted over and run through again on the opposite side; the human voices, naturally, will be speaking backwards but the paranormal voices will not.

But, as Gilbert Bonner remarked to me, 'It is clear that it is not just a matter of electronics. The human factor is involved.' Just as there is a dispute as to whether or not anyone can become a medium, so EVP researchers disagree as to whether anyone can get voices on tape. Some say that this is possible but others, like Gilbert, disagree. He claims that it requires a special sort of sensitivity.

There appears to be a connection between EVP and mediumship. A taper who is a medium is likely to get better results. It has been suggested that Raudive was a powerful medium, although he himself may not have been aware of it. It is, however, a gift of physical rather than mental mediumship that is needed. A physical medium can provide power for the communicators to draw upon and I believe that this is fundamentally the same power that is used in the manifestations of the séance room.

To what extent the mind of the taper plays a part has yet to be decided. Sarah Estep surmises that the mind acts as a sort of antenna to receive the 'signal'. In any type of mediumship, the mind of the medium is involved. Even a medium speaking in deep trance will subconsciously influence or colour the communication coming through her and this possibility cannot be entirely eliminated with EVP.

I have already mentioned the projection theory, put forward in Raudive's time and still held by many parapsychologists. According to this, all EVP voices, if they are not misinterpretations of radio emissions, are in some fashion projected onto the tape from the subconscious mind of the operator. Gilbert has come up against this attitude many times. Some years ago, he gave a demonstration of EVP to members of the Society for Psychical Research during which he recorded a number of voices, under test conditions, on a tape provided by them. All three members of the society who were present heard the voices, some of which called his name, yet they dismissed them as mere projection. While he finds this attitude exasperating, Gilbert understands why it exists.

'To accept EVP voices as genuine implies acceptance of survival. Most parapsychologists are committed to materialism so their only recourse is to deny that the voices exist or else to attribute them to the subconscious.'

For anyone who wants to try their hand at recording voices, I am now going to give a few tips. Before anyone asks me, no, I have not tried it myself, but this information has been gleaned from various tapers I have spoken to, so I offer it for what it is worth.

It is not vital to have elaborate, expensive equipment to begin with although, obviously, the better the equipment, the better the results are likely to be. However, it is important to use good quality tapes. The evening or late at night seems to be the best time for recording. Tune to a quiet spot on the dial between stations. Long, short or medium wave bands can be used. There are varying opinions as to which yield the best results. Gilbert told me that he records on the medium wave band around 1500 KHz, to a spot avoiding radio transmissions and allowing a modest input of radio 'mush' from foreign stations. He has also had some success on the short wave near to 31 or 41 metres.

Let the tape run for just a few minutes before playing it back. The reason for this is that tapes take a long time to analyse; five minutes of recording may take thirty minutes to analyse. Listen to the tape several times over using headphones as this makes the voices much easier to hear. A lot of patience is required at this stage since, if there are voices there, it is not easy to distinguish them from the background noise.

The microphone should be hand-held rather than the inbuilt type. It is essential to have a counter on the tape recorder, to enable you to locate and play back any messages you may receive. Gilbert also finds it useful to have a recorder fitted not only with a replay key but with a review key, to allow him to repeat the same part of the tape several times over in the play mode. Another useful piece of equipment is an amplifier to augment the sound of weak voices. Some operators use a diode, a type of crystal set. Raudive claims that this was the best method but it is not much used today.

Finally, one suggestion of my own. Bearing in mind the connection between EVP and physical mediumship, anyone who sits in a circle where this type of mediumship is being developed might find that such a circle creates good conditions for recording.

Whatever method you use, you will need infinite patience and acute hearing. And remember that, ultimately, the instrument is you. In this as in all types of mediumship the operator is a necessary part of the link. EVP is not a game. You will be attempting to make a link with the unseen world – with all the responsibility that this entails.

I have deliberately introduced a note of caution here because with EVP, as with all forms of communication, there are possible dangers if it is misused. The first thing to guard against is self-deception. When you are listening over and over to a tape, straining your ears for any sound which might be construed as a paranormal voice, it is obviously easy to imagine that you hear them, when in fact all you are hearing is distorted radio signals. The human mind, in any case, has a tendency to make patterns of random data, like seeing pictures in ink blots. The guidelines used by Gilbert Bonner are useful here; only accept voices that are clear (which can be heard by others as well as yourself), which call your name, or which make sensible and relevant comments.

There is also the risk of letting EVP become an obsession. Taping is a fascinating occupation and tapers become very enthusiastic about it. Spending long hours at the tape recorder, apart from putting a strain on family life, is very depleting because, as I have mentioned before, the operator's psychic energy is drawn upon. If you find yourself becoming too preoccupied with it, either stop taping altogether or leave it alone for a while until you get your life back into balance.

Another, more serious danger is that of contacting undesirable spirit entities. There is a plane of life in the spirit world which is peopled by spirits who are ignorant, deceptive or even occasionally malicious. This plane is close to the earth and can easily be contacted by those who dabble with ouija boards and the like out of idle curiosity, without knowing what they are doing. The tape-recorder can become a kind of electronic ouija board, drawing such entities like moths to a flame. Anyone who wants to try taping needs to be aware that this can happen, but it should not prevent anyone with a serious interest in EVP from experimenting. No method of communication is wrong in itself

– even the ouija board can give good results if properly used. It is the motive that counts. If you seek in love and sincerity you will attract only loving and helpful spirits. Some tapers like to start each session with a prayer which is always a good way to begin, but your attitude of mind, and your desire to seek the good, will be your protection.

Many tapers find that they pick up voices asking for help or for prayers. Raudive's voices sometimes made comments like 'we suffer' or 'we are tormented here'. This also is an intrusion from the lower levels of the spirit world. As we shall see in a later chapter, some souls become earthbound and wander around in a confused condition, trying to contact anyone who they think might be able to rescue them. If you get any such voices, remember that souls like this are not harmful, merely lost and say a prayer that they may be led into the light. Such voices seem to be heard mainly in the early stages of taping, then they fade away, to be replaced by other voices. It is as if the taper has broken through the shadowy region of the spirit world and entered into communication with a higher plane of existence.

In the mid 80s there was a new development in the field of EVP. Some researchers such as the Fischbachs claimed to be getting paranormal pictures on television and video equipment. The technique is still in its early stages but it holds out the possibility of exciting new discoveries in the future.

The British researcher, Samuel Alsop, who died a few years ago, achieved some success along these lines. His method was to wait until all the television stations had closed down for the night then to record, on video tapes, about fifteen minutes of the TV material, which amounted to just light and dark particles rushing over the screen. He would then select the first twenty frames of the pre-recorded video 'mush,' freezing and pausing between each frame, and studying the screen for any sign of a picture. If any picture, however shadowy, seemed to be present, he would then photograph the frame, develop the negative and print the plates. The images he obtained in this way were vague – as he himself admitted; they were not proof of anything, merely food for thought. However, some of them seem to show quite discernible faces.

An intriguing photograph of a face that appeared on a television screen was supplied to me by the parapsychologist and ghost hunter Richard Adamski. (See plate 6) He told me the story behind it.

Caroline, the lady seen sitting in the armchair in the photograph, was sitting late one night with her husband Willy in their home in Lincolnshire. The television was not switched on. Caroline's son-in-law, John, using a cheap instamatic camera, took a photo of Caroline with the baby on her lap. When the film was developed, they were all surprised to see the face on the television screen.

Caroline had no idea whom the face belonged to and she let the matter rest for three years. Then she heard of Richard and gave the picture to him to look at. He in turn passed it on to a friend who specializes in photographic work. He copied and analysed the picture and pronounced that he was eighty per cent sure it was genuine.

Richard arranged for a séance to be held in the room where the photograph had been taken, with Caroline and her daughter Anita among the sitters. The medium said that she could 'see' a young woman running through a cornfield clutching a dead baby in her arms, but she gave them no clue as to who the mystery woman on the television was.

Richard asked Caroline to send copies of the photograph to members of her family, to see if any of them knew who it was. Caroline's sister identified the woman as their grandmother Western, whom Caroline had only vaguely known.

The mystery seemed to be solved – but who was the young woman the medium had 'seen' running through the cornfield and was this young woman connected with the spirit photograph?

The question was finally answered when Caroline's brother died. Looking through his papers, she found a death certificate and a letter. In 1914 their mother had given birth to a baby who had been stillborn. The mother was alone at the time and became hysterical. She clutched the dead baby in her arms and ran with it to her husband, who was working in the cornfield. Richard concluded that Granny Western had been watching over her great great granddaughter and remembering the tragic birth that had taken place so many years earlier – her memory of which the medium had picked up.

It remains to be seen whether EVP will play a vital part in the future of psychical research. Certainly in its present state of development it is unlikely to gain much sympathy. It is too time-consuming, and the rewards are too meagre, to attract any but the most ardent of followers. But as for the future – who knows? It may be that, through EVP and other forms of physical mediumship, science and parascience can eventually come together and solve the enigma of the spirit world.

6 Mediums Who Heal

Being by nature a squeamish person, the thought of any kind of surgery fills me with dread, but a surgeon without medical qualifications, who operates using unsterilized instruments, and with no anaesthetic – it sounds horrific. Yet psychic surgeons do just this and claim to achieve some miraculous cures.

Psychic surgery exists mainly in Brazil and the Philippines, where it has been around for some time, though it is only in the last ten or twenty years that it has attracted the attention of the media in the west. The most famous surgeon was the Brazilian, José Arigo, who died in 1971. Arigo was uneducated and had never received any medical training, yet when in trance – his guide was a German doctor – he could diagnose and prescribe medicines with skill.

His operations, which needed a strong stomach to watch, were performed in trance and at lightning speed. Using knives, scissors or his bare hands, he would open patients' bodies and remove growths and diseased tissue. When he had finished, he simply pressed the flesh together and closed it up again, leaving no scar. The patients, who were not hypnotized, felt no pain and experienced no after-effects. Despite the unsanitary conditions, there was not a single case of blood poisoning.

Arigo was arrested more than once for illegally practising medicine but because of his great popular following he was released. He is estimated to have performed 2 million cures and never accepted payment for his work; in fact he lived in poverty. Numerous scientists and doctors from all over the world went to investigate his claims and watch him operating at point-blank range. He was photographed many times performing operations. One particularly blood-chilling photograph shows him inserting a rusty paper-knife under a patient's eyelid. None of the investigators discovered any sort of trickery or could provide an explanation for what they saw.

Since Arigo's time psychic surgery has increased in popularity and inevitably the field has been marred by frauds and charlatans. Nevertheless, researchers such as Guy Lyon Playfair who have taken the trouble to investigate first-hand have concluded that there are still some genuine surgeons around, though exactly how it works remains a mystery.

Apart from occasional visits from Brazilian and Philippino healers, psychic surgery has been almost unknown in this country, but Britain now has its own psychic surgeon in the person of Stephen Turoff. Stephen lives in a small village near Chelmsford, where he has built an extension onto his home to serve as a surgery. Hundreds of people go to visit him there. For many who have been pronounced incurable by their doctors, he is their last hope.

Born in the East End of London, Stephen became aware that there was something strange about himself when he was in his twenties, and started hearing voices in his head. Fearing that he was going mad, he went to a psychiatrist. To his surprise, the psychiatrist suggested that he might have psychic gifts. Unconvinced, he went to a Spiritualist church. As he sat there, he felt a warmth cover over him and decided that, bizarre though the whole thing seemed to him, he liked it there and would go again.

Several mediums gave him messages, telling him that he had a healing gift. One of them prophesied that he would become a full-time healer and would work abroad, which proved to be correct. He developed his healing power under the guidance of other healers in the church. In time he became so successful that he gave up his job as a carpenter to make healing his full-time work. At this stage he was working by the laying on of hands; psychic surgery was far from his thoughts. He performed his first psychic operation in 1985 – and it was as great a surprise to him as it was to his patient.

One evening he had a phone call from a friend named Linda. She had a bad back and asked Stephen if he could help. Stephen and his wife Kathy went to visit her. He asked Linda to lie down on the kitchen table. As soon as he touched her back, he sensed that the pain was caused by a stomach condition. Linda comfirmed this; an X-ray taken a little while previously had shown that she had an ovarian cyst.

'I heard a voice telling me I was going to give her a psychic operation in half an hour,' Stephen recounted the story to me. 'We were all surprised. We sat down, I had a cigarette and we talked about it. Half an hour later, I said to her, "You'd better get back on the table." I hadn't the faintest idea what I was going to do.'

As he laid his hands on the patient, he went into a trance. He knew no more until he came round to find Linda looking groggy and his wife staring at him as if he had gone mad. They told him that a spirit doctor had come through who had announced that his name was Dr Kahn. He had given Linda an invisible injection and had made an incision in her body using his hand, at the spot where the ovary was. The room had been flooded with the smell of ether, which was still lingering in the air.

Stephen didn't know what to make of this. They helped Linda off the table and onto the couch. Five minutes later she sat up, saying that the pain had gone. When she went to hospital for a further X-ray, two weeks later, the cyst had disappeared.

After that, psychic operations became a regular feature of his work. He wasn't very happy about it. 'It scared me,' he admitted, 'especially when Dr Kahn started using knives and later on, surgical instruments. I was always in a deep trance. I never knew what was going on.' But the results, and the gratitude of the patients he successfully treated, encouraged him to continue.

He now regularly travels abroad to demonstrate his healing gift, always accompanied by Kathy, who works with him and is herself a healer and medium. So far they have visited Spain, Sweden, Portugal and Mexico and he has had invitations to work in China and Malaysia. In Mexico he successfully treated the Chief of Police who, as Stephen remarked, is a good man to have on your side!

Spain is the country to which he returns most often and where he feels he achieves the best results. 'The people are more open,' he explained. 'They have a greater acceptance of healing than people in this country and a more reverent attitude towards it.' Some years ago he opened a small clinic at Fuengirola, on land which he bought with a Spanish friend. Later, they discovered that the place was known locally as the Hill of Miracles. The area was remote, requiring considerable effort just to get there, but since the clinic has opened, roads have been built and amenities laid on. He visits the clinic several times a year, seeing thirty or forty patients a day. When he is away, other healers are in attendance. His plan is to provide accommodation where patients who have come long distances can be put up and eventually, he would like to open an orphanage there.

Stephen knows little about his healing guide except that his name was Joseph Kahn and that he was a German Jew who died around the beginning of the century. He does not feel the need to trace him and Dr Kahn himself says that he prefers to be known by his works. The spirit doctor has, however, been seen by a number of patients, including a Roman Catholic bishop and has sometimes appeared at patients' bedsides. When Stephen is in a trance, he is completely taken over by him. His mannerisms become those of a much older man with a gruff, forthright personality and he speaks broken English with a German accent quite unlike his usual Cockney. His face is transfigured and sometimes it is possible to see Dr Kahn's dark hair and beard.

Dr Kahn was a small man, which causes problems for Stephen, who is tall and well built: 'When I'm in trance I literally shrink. My trouser legs have to be rolled up so that I don't trip over!'

According to Dr Kahn, a team of about fifteen doctors is involved in the healing. One of them, a Dr Gino, speaks fluent Italian through Stephen when he entrances him. There is a homeopath who gives advice on treatment, an osteopath who works on patients' backs when necessary, and a nurse who used to assist Dr Kahn when they were on earth.

Stephen does not perform operations on every patient; sometimes the simple laying of hands is all that is needed. He is the first to admit that not all the operations are successful. 'There is no magic wand. Sometimes more than one session of healing is needed. Sometimes there's no result at all. But if it's meant to be, it happens.'

He treats all kinds of conditions; occasionally animals too are brought to him and he has many testimonials from patients and doctors testifying to the effectiveness of his healing. The results are inexplicable by any rational means. To give just a few examples; one woman who came to him needed a hysterectomy. Following Stephen's healing she went back to her doctor who examined her and asked what other doctor she had been to; the operation had already been done. Another woman came with a brain tumour so large that it couldn't be operated upon by conventional means. She had a psychic operation during which Stephen (or Dr Kahn) told her to return a week later for further treatment. The woman failed to do so. However, when she was examined in hospital it was found that three quarters of the tumour had gone, and there was a hole where it had been.

A man was brought to Stephen's house in a car because he was too ill to drive; he was suffering from a tumour on the spine. After the operation he was well enough to drive home and an X-ray examination confirmed that the tumour had gone. A Church of England vicar brought a patient in a wheelchair, suffering from a brain tumour. Ten minutes later, the patient got up and walked – and the vicar ran out terrified!

I myself watched Stephen working, when he came to do a healing demonstration at Wimbledon Church. He worked in front of about three hundred people, including many members of the public who had come in, having seen the event advertised in the local paper. Nothing was hidden. Before he started, he invited anyone who wished to come up and examine the instruments he was going to use and during the demonstration several people from the audience were permitted to stand close to him.

Stephen performed several operations, including one on a lady called Wilma suffering from a stomach ulcer and one on a patient called Françoise, who was suffering from back pain due to a deformity she had had since she was a child. Françoise told me, 'I felt Stephen make an incision in my spine, like an acupuncture needle, then there was a sensation like a larger instrument going in, I felt him chipping away at the bone at the base of the pelvis. There was no pain. He said he was drawing out the poison. I felt a drawing sensation that started at the tips of my fingers and went up my arms into my back.'

Stephen then manipulated her back with what appeared to the audience like horrifying violence. When he had finished, he told her to touch her toes.

'I was able to do it – it was the first time I had touched my toes in years!'

At the time of writing, some months after the healing, both Wilma and Françoise are still free of pain.

Even if you have witnessed it first-hand, psychic surgery takes some believing. So how does it work? Stephen admits that he is not sure, but he speculates that it may be connected with the mechanism by which physical mediumship operates. Before he begins work he often feels ectoplasm coming out of his hands and it would seem that this is what the spirit doctors use to work with.

'Dr Kahn has told me that they build a field of radiation around the body and work within that. They provide some means of sterilizing the instruments. Very few operations actually go into the body and, if any incisions are made, they are no more than an inch or so long. The instruments seem to be lengthened – extended – within the body using the ectoplasm.'

This view is supported by patients who claim to have felt sensations within the body even if no incisions had been made at all. Others say that they can feel hands inside them, while Stephen's hands are only resting lightly on top of the body. As with Arigo, when incisions are made, the flow of blood is minimal which is just as well, since Stephen admits that he cannot stand the sight of blood! The wound closes up in seconds, leaving only a red line which fades in an hour or so.

Sometimes the tumour or diseased matter appears through the skin, without any incision being made. The lumps seem to be dematerialized then rematerialized outside. Patients are offered the gory tokens to take away and have analysed if they wish. If not, they are placed in a dish and later disposed of, though Stephen says that they sometimes just disappear of their own accord.

The manipulation of limbs, Stephen believes, is done by the spirit doctors softening the bones then realigning them. Many patients, like Françoise, have been cured of painful back conditions. In Spain, a young boy was brought to Stephen who had one leg one and a half inches shorter than the other. After the treatment, the shorter leg had grown to the same length as the normal one.

Ether is often smelt while the operations are taking place. Stephen claims that patients are anaesthetized by invisible injections and many have reported feeling the prick of a needle and becoming drowsy. It is rare for anyone to complain of pain though certain operations, particularly on the eye and sinuses, may cause discomfort.

Stephen is convinced that the operations are frequently

carried out more to convince the patient that healing has taken place than because they are necessary to bring about a cure. Dr Kahn has told him, 'Seeing is believing in your world today; people need to see.' However the spirit doctor claims that, in some cases, quicker results are obtained through this method than through contact healing alone.

But the real healing, according to Stephen, takes place on a higher level than the physical. 'There is a lot going on that's not seen. The work starts even before the patient lays down and continues afterwards. It's not just the body that's being healed, it's the whole person.'

He finds that his work is constantly changing and becoming more physical. A recent development has been the production of oil from his hands. Patients and onlookers have been told by Dr Kahn to rub the oil into their hands and think of a perfume. Two or three minutes later, the oil has changed into that scent.

Stephen willingly co-operates with doctors and allows them to watch him working. At a recent seminar of the World Congress of Natural Medicines in Spain he demonstrated before sixty doctors, who were invited to observe him at close quarters and to inspect the instruments he used. Not surprisingly, he finds that doctors as a whole view him with grave suspicion. This often changes if they see him working for themselves, and in fact some doctors have referred patients to him.

Other members of the medical profession, however, are determinedly hostile and refuse to look at the evidence. When one woman who was enabled to walk after seven years in a wheelchair told her doctor of the healing she had received his reaction was, 'There couldn't have been anything wrong with you in the first place!'

Stephen also encounters some hostility from other healers who are suspicious of his methods or consider them too sensational. He is aware of the dangers of pyschic surgery in the wrong hands; fraudulent healers or even those who are sincerely motivated but lack the necessary gift. He is also aware of the danger to himself of being accused of doing a patient harm, but this is a risk he is prepared to take. In fact, in all the years he has been healing he has only had two complaints of adverse results, and neither complaint was substantiated.

He believes that there will be more psychic surgeons in the future and that this form of healing, though to many it strains their credulity too far, will gain wider acceptance.

'Some of the cases I get are heartbreaking, particularly the children, and I have to come to terms with the fact that not everyone can be healed. But I love my work. When I'm healing, I feel a oneness with everything. I *am* the trees, the flowers, the birds. I love God with all my heart and I think I'm so privileged to have been chosen to heal in this way.'

Another healer, Geoff Boltwood, has recently begun to move into the area of psychic surgery. Geoff became aware of his healing mission at an early age. When he was five he was in hospital with rheumatic fever. When the illness was at its height he saw a light which appeared by the bed and heard a voice saying, 'You will get better and you will heal others.'

He made a swift recovery, but after he returned home he discovered that he had changed. The light seemed to have entered into him, giving him an abundance of psychic energy. There was an outbreak of poltergeist activity in his home. Lights turned themselves on and off or fused. He was too young to analyse what had happened and was amused rather than frightened by it. He was able to make small objects jump and this became a game to him. Once, he showed a school-friend, who was horrified, and after this he kept it to himself. He also became clairvoyant and was able to see spirit people as if they were solid figures. Fortunately, his mother understood and encouraged his gift.

During his teens his clairvoyant ability lessened. When he decided to develop as a medium, he had to work at it to get it back again. In his early twenties he began practising as a healer. Like Stephen, he started by doing contact healing and this is still the main part of his work, but a few years ago, when he was giving a healing demonstration at the Spiritualist church in Swindon, he realized that something stranger was happening.

'Ash was literally pouring off my hands. I'd never experienced anything like it before. People said it resembled the healing ash or vibhutti that is produced by the Indian guru, Sai Baba.'

Later, there was another development. Instead of ash, oil began to appear. The oil now appears quite often when he is working. Sometimes it comes in great quantities; as much as a bowlful. Patients report that this oil has a healing quality when rubbed into the skin. It has a strong smell that lingers for a long time. One patient who was unfamiliar with Geoff's healing methods thought he was using powerful aftershave! She could still smell it, three days and several baths after the healing session. The oil has been tested by scientists, who have concluded only that it is 'of organic origin'.

Like Stephen, Geoff had no idea of taking up psychic surgery but he found, much to his own surprise, that he would occasionally be entranced by his guides while healing and operations would be performed. One of his first patients was a woman suffering from back pain which was caused by fibrous tissue which was too close to the spine to be operated upon by normal means. He noticed, as Stephen had commented, that the lump apparently materialized.

'I laid my hands on her back. In a couple of minutes a piece of tissue appeared. It didn't come out of the body in the usual way, it seemed to appear outside. She was instantly able to walk, free from pain.'

Geoff has taken part in a number of experiments designed to test the effectiveness of healing. In 1989 a series of tests was devised by Dr Tony Schofield and Dr David Hodges of the University of London, to measure the healer's ability to stimulate the germination and growth of cress seeds. The seeds were first 'stressed' by being soaked in a salt solution. Under normal circumstances, the seeds would recover from the effects of the solution within a few days but the scientists wanted to find out whether, with healing, they would recover more quickly. Geoff was allowed to hold the seeds in his hands while he directed healing energy to them. Another control group of seeds received no healing.

The results obtained were very positive. The seeds that had not received healing developed slowly. Those that had, germinated immediately and grew rapidly. The report, printed in the *Journal* of the Society for Psychical Research stated that 'the healing treatment appeared to have accelerated germination considerably in some seeds, an increase in the region of several hundred-fold.' The report also noted that the seeds grew and developed steadily in a balanced way, 'such that an initial growth rate was followed by an even development of both root and shoot'; an indication of the claim that has always been made by healers that healing brings the organism in to a state of balance.

Geoff was instructed to wash his hands in distilled water before handling each batch of seeds and was carefully observed to see that he did not cheat in any way. The scientists conducting the experiment were fully satisfied as to his integrity. They concluded;

> We believe that using the experimental model we can demonstrate that the healing effect exists and that we have done so in this particular case. The model is flexible and capable of modification and we propose to overcome any potential criticisms of the method used here and extend its use to other healers. Nevertheless, although we consider that the results obtained do support the contention that a healing ability exists, it is unlikely that any laboratory model will ever satisfy those who do not wish to know.

Their last remark was well founded. Scientists are notorious for having closed minds regarding anything that upsets their preconceived theories. One scientist claimed that Geoff must have hypnotized the two doctors and the other observers into believing that the seeds had germinated!

Geoff does not let such criticism discourage him. Though he is willing to co-operate with scientists and doctors, he prefers to spend his time actually healing. In common with Stephen, he says that his gift is constantly changing and developing and he readily admits that healing is not successful in every case.

He believes that psychic surgery will become a larger part of his work but he shares Stephen's view that the removal of tissue may be done more to convince the patient than because it is a vital part of the cure. He also agrees with Stephen that the real healing takes place on a spiritual dimension; this is one of the reasons why it is so hard for scientists to analyse.

'You can't just remove the lump, you also have to heal at this higher level, otherwise you are just treating the symptoms, not removing the underlying cause.'

Treating the whole person is the basis of spiritual healing. Like other forms of alternative and complementary medicine, it recognizes that man is composed of mind, body and spirit and aims to treat all three, bringing the entire being into a state of harmony and wholeness.

Spiritual healing is often confused with faith healing but they are not the same. Faith healing, by definition, depends upon the patient's faith in the healer. Spiritual healing can be effective even when the person concerned does not know they are receiving healing. It can be used on animals as well as people and, most surprisingly, it can operate over any distance. Healers are often asked to send healing thoughts and prayers to patients who cannot visit them personally and this absent, or distant healing, can work just as well as the laying on of hands.

Healers claim that they do nothing of themselves. They are simply channels for healing energy, which they see as a universal God-given power. As one healer explained to me, 'The power is all around us. Healers are people who have been born with the capacity to open themselves to it and to transmit it to others, like a transformer. As it flows into the patient it has a cleansing effect. It removes mental and physical blocks and stimulates the body to heal itself.'

Healing is completely non-denominational and healers are drawn from all faiths and religions. People who call themselves spiritual healers are not necessarily Spiritualists, but those who are, work like mediums, with the assistance of guides. Many of these guides were doctors and nurses when on earth and are continuing their healing mission from the other side of life.

Most of the healers I have met, like most of the mediums, seem very ordinary people on the surface, but occasionally I have come across one who positively exudes psychic energy. The healer Barrie Redington is one of these. Barrie is a very down-to-earth, even blunt person and used to be a market trader before taking up healing full-time, but when I met him I was immediately aware of the power that radiates from him like a strong force-field. I was not surprised to learn that his patients often say they feel a surge of energy when he places his hands upon them, but this energy caused Barrie a lot of problems in his younger days.

When he was in his twenties he was involved in a serious motor accident which left him with head injuries. For a long time afterwards he suffered aches and pains and erratic mood swings even though medically he appeared to have made a full recovery. Eventually he learned, through coming into contact with mediums and healers, that the pains were due to the excessive amount of energy which was pouring through him and was out of control. The power sometimes manifested itself in embarrassing ways, causing various phenomena in his home and outside. When he and his wife Susan ate out in restaurants, spoons and forks would bend. Susan would frantically try to straighten them out before the waiters saw them! When he trained as a healer and learned to channel the power correctly, the manifestations ceased and his physical symptoms cleared up.

Barrie never seeks publicity but his work has attracted the attention of journalists. One of them, Jack Pleasant, who writes on the paranormal, investigated the case of a woman who went to Barrie with a lump in the breast which the doctors had advised her to have removed for an exploratory operation. While having healing, the patient felt mildly nauseous. When she returned home she was physically sick and vomited up a black fibrous ball the size of a golf ball. When she felt for the lump, she found it had gone.

After Barrie was featured in the magazine *TV Quick* he found himself inundated with requests for help. Among those who had healing from him following the article was a man suffering from AIDS. 'When he first came,' Barrie told me, 'he was at death's door. Now, though he's not actually cured of the disease, he has so much energy that he's able to work a hundred hours a week at his business. The doctors can't believe what's happened to him.'

Barrie has two healing guides, a Welsh surgeon, Dr Jones, and a German doctor, Heinrich Lahmann. Through information he was given clairvoyantly, Barrie was able to verify that a Dr Lahmann lived in Heidelburg in the last century and was a pioneer of homeopathy. Barrie says that it is the guides who do the real work – he is just the instrument.

If he cannot visit a patient personally, he sends them one of his healing cloths. These are strips of wool which he has held in his hands, concentrating his energy into them. Many sufferers have gained relief by wearing these cloths or pressing them against the part of the body affected.

Claims of miracle cures may be hard to believe, but they do sometimes happen. Usually, however, healing is a gradual process, possibly requiring many sessions. It should also be said that healing sometimes does not work at all. In some cases it may achieve a partial result, alleviating the condition without curing it, or giving only temporary relief. But most patients receive some benefit, even if it is only increased peace of mind and strength to cope with the illness – and that is more than orthodox medicine can offer.

Doctors have always been sceptical of healing but there are signs today that the medical profession as a whole is beginning to adopt a more open-minded attitude. Many scientific tests like the ones in which Geoff Boltwood participated have been carried out, and these have indicated the ability of healers not only to affect the growth of plants, but to bring about other effects for which science has no explanation. For instance, healing has been shown to be able to alter the composition of water, to strengthen the immune system, reduce tension and anxiety and hasten the healing of wounds in people and animals.

In an experiment conducted in California by Dr Daniel Worth and screened on the BBC2 series *Your Life in Their Hands*, a team of volunteers were each given a wound in the upper arm. Half of them were then given treatment by a healer without their knowledge. After sixteen days, thirteen of the group of twenty-three were completely healed, the other ten were well on the way to recovery. The wounds on the control group who received no healing had not cleared up.

Experiments such as these, which rule out the theory that healing is all in the patient's mind, have encouraged doctors to take the subject seriously. An increasingly large number of doctors now refer their patients to healers. A few years ago Dr Daniel Benor set up the Doctor-Healer Network, an organization which enables doctors and healers to meet together regularly to discuss how they can co-operate with each other. Government legislation now permits a doctor registered with the General Medical Council to use or prescribe healing, provided that the doctor remains in charge of the case and continues to give medical treatment as necessary.

Healers for their part are keen to co-operate with doctors. Ten years ago, the Confederation of Healing Organisations was formed with the aim of improving the status of healing by bringing together the various healing organizations under one umbrella and providing doctors with a corpus of recognized healers whom they could trust. At present, healers are admitted to NHS hospitals at the request of patients, but it is the ambition of the CHO to establish healing as a standard therapy for the NHS as well as private practice. The CHO is also setting up a series of clinical trials to test the ways in which healing can be of benefit.

The CHO is completely non-denominational and its members are drawn from all religions, including Spiritualism. It co-operates with medical bodies such as the Council for Alternative and Complementary Medicine as well as organizations offering different types of therapy. All healers within the CHO are bound by a Code of Conduct which was drawn up in such a way as to make it acceptable to doctors. No precise method of healing is laid down in the code but members are urged to avoid techniques which may invite ridicule, to behave with dignity, courtesy, discretion and tact, not to give medical diagnoses and not to countermand instructions given by a doctor.

Slowly the CHO is achieving its aims. The Code of Conduct has been welcomed by leading medical authorities such as the British Medical Association, the Royal College of Nursing and the Royal College of Physicians. Fifteen hospitals have agreed to co-operate with the CHO's healing service for people with AIDS and cancer and one quarter of all Family Practitioner Committees and Primary Care Divisions have agreed to distribute the CHO's offer of a healing service to their thousands of GPs.

The value of healing is not limited to physical illnesses. It can also promote inner peace and relaxation and relieve stress. There are a number of small retreat houses and healing sanctuaries around the country which provide accommodation, where people can stay for a few days to unwind and recharge their batteries.

Medium Eddie Burks, who was featured in my last book for his 'rescue work', which he still does, runs one such retreat centre. Called Inlight House, it is in a tranquil setting on the borders of Surrey and Hampshire. All sorts of people go there, but the centre caters especially for those who care for others, the sick or the elderly, who may be in need of rest and healing themselves, and for cancer sufferers (although it cannot accommodate those who are in need of constant medical attention).

Eddie finds that people become more open to spiritual

healing through being able to relax. 'The experience of healing seems to open them to a greater consciousness of the spiritual side of things. It often releases a lot of pent-up emotion which may be the root cause of the physical symptoms.'

So spiritual healing is a very valuable therapy for all kinds of conditions. There are healers attached to every Spiritualist church and centre and the National Federation of Spiritual Healers, whose address is given at the back of this book, is always pleased to put patients in touch with healers in their area.

It should be stressed that healing should not be regarded as an alternative to orthodox medicine but rather as a complement to it. The two should work together to bring about a speedier and more complete cure. Healing is often used as a last resort in cases where medical science can do no more, but it is better to seek help at the onset of an illnes than to wait until the case is desperate, by which time healing may not work or may take a long time. It is never too late, however. Some people diagnosed as incurable by doctors have made remarkable recoveries and, even if this is not possible, healing can relieve suffering and help the patient to pass out of life peacefully, without pain.

'Spiritual healing,' as one of Stephen's grateful patients remarked to me, 'is one of God's most precious gifts.' It is good that it is at last beginning to receive the recognition it deserves.

7 Ghosts Are People

The house in which I grew up was haunted. It was a large, eighteenth century house with a cellar and an attic and a number of rooms that had been shut up for years and not used; just the sort of place where you would expect a ghost to walk.

From the time my family and I moved in – I was about three years old – it was obvious that there was something not right about it. Footsteps would be heard in the upstairs rooms when there was no one there. My uncle Harry, who lived with us, complained that he constantly felt someone standing behind him. Sometimes at night we were awakened by the sound of breaking glass. My mother would rush downstairs, fearing that a burglar had broken in. ('Don't go down there by yourself,' my father would say wisely, 'take Harry with you'.) But when they got there they never found any signs of damage, although the dog would be cowering in a corner, shivering with fear and would run out of the room with its tail between its legs.

All this happened when I was too young to take much notice. It wasn't until I was in my teens, by which time my latent gift of mediumship had begun to develop, that I saw the ghost. It was a little old lady with white hair, wearing a long, black dress. I only caught a fleeting glimpse of her out of the corner of my eye and when I turned my head to look, she had vanished. It all happened too quickly for me to be frightened. After that, I glimpsed her on a number of occasions. Though I could never hold her in my field of vision or make any contact with her, I somehow formed the impression that she had been the housekeeper there in former days. Several times I saw her, in the traditional manner of ghosts, walking through the wall. The house had been substantially altered by the previous owner and there wouldn't have been a wall in that position in her time. As the years passed her appearances grew less frequent until they faded away altogether.

The other disturbances stopped too. I never did discover the cause of them, but all the time I lived there, I felt invisible presences around me. They were not frightening but, all the same, it was not a comfortable atmosphere for a psychic and highly sensitive child to grow up in.

Ghosts are very common. In my work as a medium, I have come across hundreds of hauntings, from the wispy figures in white robes variety to the puzzling and often frightening activities of poltergeists. The subject is a complicated one. Each case needs to be examined carefully to see what is behind it and there is no one explanation that can account for them all.

It is generally assumed, when they are given any credence at all, that ghosts are the spirits of the departed returning to haunt the houses where they used to live. This may sometimes be so, but not in every instance. Longfellow expressed a truth when he wrote, 'All houses where in men have lived and died are haunted houses.' Strong emotions or traumatic events have a way of impressing themselves into the very walls and fabric of a building, so that a sensitive person can pick up those impressions, see the people of the past and watch the events being re-enacted, like a video being replayed. This may well explain the sound of breaking glass in my parents' house.

The traditional hooded monks and white ladies with their heads tucked underneath their arms are usually ghosts of this type. One has to say 'usually' because in the world of the supernatural, nothing can be taken for granted. These are ghosts in the true sense of the word; not mere wraiths or memory traces. They always appear in the same place and carry out the same actions, like obsessive sleep-walkers. Any attempt to contact them is futile because they are in reality no more than shells. The spirit of the person they once were has passed on to a higher level of existence.

The Long Gallery at Hampton Court provides an example of such a haunting. It was through this gallery that the fifth wife of Henry VIII, Katherine Howard, ran screaming to the chapel where the king was at prayer, in a desperate attempt to plead for her life. Those screams have been heard many times and several residents of the palace have seen her white figure gliding down the gallery.

A few years ago, a man working in a cellar in York saw a

whole legion of Roman soldiers come marching through the wall. Terrified though he was, he kept his wits sufficiently to notice what they were wearing. On checking later with an historian, it was found that the details of the costume he described were correct for the period.

Phantoms like this have no more substance than a picture on a cinema screen. They can be temporarily reanimated by a medium or a person with psychic energy coming into their vicinity, which gives them a brief semblance of life, but it is no more than a semblance. We should not imagine that Katherine Howard spends her afterlife running up and down the gallery of Hampton Court for the benefit of tourists or that the Roman legions march eternally through the streets of York. In time, these forms like my ghost of the little old lady, will fade away and be seen no more.

Ghosts have occasionally been captured by the camera. *Photographing the Spirit World* by Cyril Permutt contains some fascinating examples. One intriguing photograph was supplied to me by Reg Wickens, a retired quality control technician from Frome in Somerset. One warm summer day Reg took a snapshot of the local Morton House guest-house because he was attracted to the floral display outside. After taking a close-up he crossed the road to take a large picture from the other side of the street. 'I had some sort of feeling,' he said later, 'that something was urging me across.'

When the prints were developed he was amazed to see the misty figure of a motor-cyclist, complete with goggles, leather helmet and long, black mac. The photographs were published in the local paper and drew a response from a retired postman, Graham Sturgess. According to Mr Sturgess, during the Second World War military motor-cyclists had used that road, which was near to Field Marshall Montgomery's headquarters. One of them, he recalled, had swerved and crashed into the wall opposite what is now the guest-house.

'The more I think of it,' Reg told me, 'the more I am convinced that the day I took the photo was the anniversary of the rider's death.'

Even this figure, which in the photograph appears larger than life, is probably no more than a memory impressed onto the atmosphere by the intensity of the rider's fear as he crashed. But earthbound souls there undoubtedly are; souls who, for one reason or another, have become trapped in the places they knew, unable to leave them. These are the ghosts of many haunted houses. They can terrify anyone who happens to catch a glimpse of them, but nearly always they are harmless. If they create a disturbance, it is not done to cause fear, but is an attempt to attract attention to themselves and appeal for help.

For the plight of such a soul is a desperately unhappy one. Caught between two worlds, belonging neither to one nor the other, they are lost and confused, living in a kind of dream world from which they are unable to awake. They are so closely tied to the earth that, strange though it may seem, they may not even realize they are dead. They are unaware of the existence of a spirit realm, and cannot see other spirit people. If they do see them, they assume *they* are ghosts! For this reason, it is difficult for anyone from that side of life to get through to them, but a medium, because he is still in the physical body, may be able to reach them more easily. Often a brief contact is all that is needed to make them aware of their situation. Once this has been achieved, the medium's spirit helpers can take over and lead them away to where they can be taken care of.

One medium who is well-known for this rescue work, as it is called, is Philip Steff. Philip lives in Bath. When not rescuing lost souls he earns his living as a carpark attendant. Over the course of the last twenty years he has dealt with some sixty cases, of which he claims that all but one have been completely successful.

When Philip is called in to investigate a haunting he takes one or two colleagues with him, who are usually mediums themselves, to record what happens and to assist by providing psychic power. He invites the people living in the house to join in the resuce if they wish, explaining to them that there is nothing to be afraid of. He then walks around the house until he locates the 'cold spot'; this place is the focus of the psychic energy. Then he goes into trance and allows his guide to speak through him to the haunting spirits, telling them that they are in the wrong dimension and must leave.

'I tell them to go towards the light,' Philip explained to me, using a phrase that is frequently employed by mediums. By 'the light', they mean the spiritual light that is brought by the spirit guides and is invisible to those on earth. For the distressed soul, this appears as a comforting glow in the dark, confused state in

Linda Williamson

Psychic drawing by Rita Taylor and (*inset*) photograph of the same
man in real life

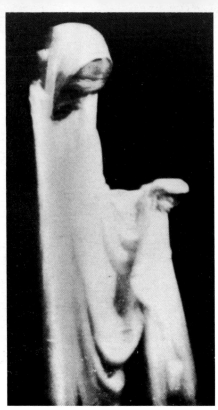

A materialized figure at a Helen Duncan séance

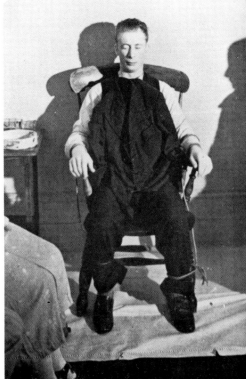

Jack Webber, showing the removal of his coat

Minnie Harrison using ectoplasm to manipulate a trumpet

The ghost on the television screen

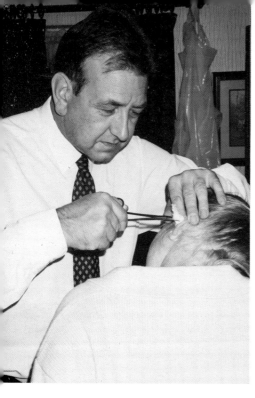

Stephen Turoff working on a patient

The ghostly motor-cyclist photographed by Reg Wickens

which they are existing. As a man who is lost on a dark night will follow the light of a friendly lantern, so they can follow this light until it leads them into the higher dimension of the spirit world where they belong. And here, their own loved ones, who may well have been trying unsuccessfully to reach them, will be waiting to greet them.

'I feel a great sense of joy and relief as they leave,' Philip said. 'I sense their emotion. Sometimes they've been in this earthbound condition for years and when they're released, it's like being let out of prison.'

It's a great relief too, for the haunted family who, if they are sensitive, are aware that the atmosphere has lightened when the spirit has gone. Not everyone, however, is pleased. Some people rather like their ghosts and want to hold onto them. Philip thinks this cruel.

'Ghosts are people. The spirit trapped there is a real person. They should be helped, not allowed to go on suffering.'

It is not only old houses that are haunted. Philip has been called to investigate flats in modern high-rise blocks, pubs and office premises. He was once called out to a restaurant where the owner complained of an atrocious smell beneath one of his tables which all the usual cleaning methods had failed to dislodge. Philip traced the trouble to a woman who had lived there in squalor and had died in the 1700s.

The restaurant owner was sceptical; but had to admit that, after Philip's visit, the smell vanished.

The reason why a soul may become earthbound are many. Traditional ghost stories about spirits who cannot rest because of their earthly misdeeds or because of some unfinished business contain more than a germ of truth. A person who has been completely attached to material things may find it impossible to leave them behind and move onto a spiritual dimension of existence. As the Bible says, 'Where your treasure is, there will your heart be also.' Such a spirit could continue to inhabit the house where they used to live, not realizing that they are dead and regarding the new occupants as intruders.

Suicide is one of the most common causes of a soul being in an earthbound condition. Those who take their own lives often feel bitter regret and find that, far from having solved their problems, they have landed themselves in a worse mess than they were in before. This is not invariably the case, however.

Much depends on the motive. A person who killed themselves because of mental instability, for instance, or because of extreme pain, would not suffer in the same way as a person who had committed suicide as a cowardly way out of a difficult situation. There is love and compassion in the spirit world for every soul that arrives there but someone who went over in a distressed mental condition would be hard to help, in the same way that, in this life, someone who shuts themselves in mentally because of depression is hard for others to get through to.

Souls in an earthbound state can impinge upon the minds of the living. People living in a haunted house can pick up the emotions of the spirit trapped there and become anxious, irritable or depressed for no apparent reason. This I discovered when I was called in to investigate a house in South London which was haunted by the spirit of a boy who had taken his own life.

One day I had a phone call from a woman called Susan. Her teenage daughter Sharon had seen the ghost of a young man on the stairs of their house and was terrified. Could I go over there and see if there was anything I could do?

When I arrived at the house, both mother and daughter were in a state of anxiety. They told me that, ever since they had moved in there they had both felt uncomfortable and had suffered from unaccountable bouts of depression. The family had previously been a happy one, but now they were all at loggerheads with each other. Susan believed that the ghost was having an evil influence on them all.

I sat in Sharon's bedroom, where she said she had often felt the boy's presence. It wasn't long before I became aware of him. He was about twenty, an ordinary modern boy in a white shirt and jeans. I described what I saw to Sharon and she nodded with relief; at least she was reassured that she wasn't having hallucinations, or, if she was, I was sharing them too.

It took me some time to get through to the boy. Earthbound spirits, because of their mental state, are hard to contact clearly – but, speaking to him in my mind, I gathered that he had been on drugs, and had killed himself in a moment of depression by taking an overdose. He was not malicious and did not intend any harm to the family; quite the reverse, in fact. He had a sympathetic feeling towards Sharon because she was roughly the same age as himself and he had attached himself to her

because she was the only member of the family psychic enough
to be able to see him.

I directed my thoughts towards him, telling him to leave the
house and go with the my spirit helpers, who would look after
him, but when I went away I knew that my task hadn't been
completed. I sensed that I had made some progress and helped
to lighten the darkness of his mind but I knew that he still hadn't
detached himself completely from his earthly conditions.

During the next few days I kept him in my thoughts and
prayers, asking for him to be released, and I asked several of my
medium friends to do the same. Then a few nights later, I had a
phone call from Susan.

'He's gone, hasn't he?' she asked.

'I can't tell,' I told her truthfully.

'I'm sure he has,' she replied, and told me her story.

That day she had gone to work as usual, but during the course
of the morning she had felt unwell. She couldn't say exactly
what was wrong but it had been so bad that her employers had
sent her home. When she reached the house she sat down
quietly and, as she rested, she felt the boy come very close,
overshadowing her. For a few minutes she was overwhelmed by
his emotions. She felt his remorse at having taken his own life
and felt too that he wanted to say he was sorry for the trouble he
had caused in the family.

She spoke to him mentally, telling him that she forgave him
and telling him to go forward into the light. Then, as suddenly
as it had descended, the depression lifted and was replaced by
elation. She knew he had gone.

'It's a happy house now,' she told me. The spirit of the boy
had been released and he had left a blessing behind him.

It is hard to imagine the state of mind of a soul caught in this
condition, but fascinating insight is provided by Matthew
Manning's book *The Strangers*. Matthew became famous while
in his teens for his psychic and telekenetic ability; he was
Britain's answer to Uri Geller. These days, Matthew channels
his energies into healing but in 1978, when the book was
written, he was still at school.

Matthew lived with his parents and sister in an eighteenth
century house in Cambridgeshire. He first became aware that it
was haunted when he saw at the top of the stairs a man in

eighteenth century dress, supporting himself on two sticks. He guessed that it must be Robert Webbe, a corn merchant who had built the house and died there in 1733.

There was a considerable amount of poltergeist activity, some of it involving the movement of heavy items of furniture, but Matthew found that this activity lessened when he allowed Webbe to communicate with him through automatic writing. This, apparently, gave Webbe the opportunity he needed to make contact with a mind outside his own.

Matthew had undertaken a school project to write a history of the house and neighbourhood and Webbe decided to give him some assistance. Names started to appear, written on the walls, doors and ceilings of the house. 'I did see your owne fine workes on my familye,' Webbe wrote through Matthew's hand, 'and did decide to helpe you by allowing my frendes to sign their names on the wall.' Webbe promised 'half of a thousand names' and he kept his word. Hundreds of different signatures appeared over the course of a few weeks and many of the names were able to be traced through the parish registers of the seventeenth and eighteenth centuries.

Webbe's troubled state of mind emerges through the writing. At times he seems to be still living his life in the eighteenth century, sharing the house with his own family, carrying on his business, seeing his friends, and constantly complaining of gout. He writes:

> A mightey fine daye and off to myne man Rob: Moore for a fine goodley meel with myne wyfe. And just too church today and a boring sermon. Didst tickel myne fancey to have a taste of licker in the sermon. And myne man Browne is such a fool. Just last week did he lose his roofe to flames. A mightey fyne fire. I didst stand and watch but not to close lest my pretty wig by lycked by the flames.

When asked what date it is, he invariably gives some date between 1726 and 1733. Yet sometimes he indicates that he is aware that he is dead. He writes at one point,

> I died in 1733 from my troublesome legs.

He is dimly aware of Matthew and his family but still complains. 'This is my house.' He sees things that belong to the present day, such as the family car, but is unable to understand anything that would not have existed in his own time. Sometimes there is a curious time-slip effect, as when Matthew finds a loaf on the stairs which Webbe claimed his servant baked for him.

Webbe claims not to believe in life after death and, when Matthew challenges him, telling him he is a ghost, he becomes confused and frightened.

'Have you ever seen a ghost?' I wrote.

'No, I believe not. And goode, too.'

'What would you do if you *did* see one?'

'I would tell it that it was not real and that I was Robert Webbe.'

'Are there ghosts in your house?' I asked, beginning to realise that some fascinating material was likely to be written if I asked the right question.

'Of course not else I would chase them away,' he quickly replied.

'We live in your house now and we have seen a ghost here.'

'I do not believe such tales. You try to frighten me out.'

'The ghost we have seen wears breeches, stockings, a long coat, waistcoat, and wig. He has two sticks and appears on the stairs,' I informed him.

'But I never see any ghost in myne house. Do you speak with this ghoull or is it dumb?' He asked apparently completely unaware that I was referring to *him*.

'We speak with it,' I told him.

'But how speke you with it if it is dead? The dead cannot talk. But tell me a little of what this ghoul says.'

'He tells us that he lived in this house and that he died in 1733.'

'This cannot be so,' he replied indignantly in automatic writing. 'I live here if 'tis 1733. And I am not a ghoul. I am Rob: Webbe. And tell me what this ghost is called?'

'He calls himself Robert Webbe,' I told him.

'But this cannot be. I am Rob: Webbe. You have a man who cheets you. I am Rob: W. And you have too someone who likes to be me. Off with you. I am here and I am me.'

Matthew asks him who he thinks he is talking to.

'I think sometimes I am going mad. I hear a voice in my head which I hear talking to me and asking what I do. But tell no one else they locke me away ... Who are you? Are you the ghost this voyce talks of?'

And he asks Matthew. 'Are you a ghoulle of tomorrow?'

Let us try to unravel what is happening here. Webbe was apparently not a particularly bad man, but he was completely selfish and materialistic. All his thoughts were centred on his wealth and the fine house he had built for himself so that, when he died, he was unable to detach himself from them.

Everyone, when they die, enters the spirit or astral world. This world has many different levels, ranging from the levels that are still very close to earth – and resemble the earth in many ways – to spheres of consciousness which are so elevated as to be beyond our understanding. We will explore this concept of the different spheres in more detail in a later chapter. For the time being, suffice it to say that Webbe is living on one of the lowest planes which interpenetrate the physical plane. He is in fact occupying the same physical space as when he was alive, but in a different dimension – only he has not fully grasped that he had made the transition from one dimension to another.

He is inhabiting his own mental world, like a person living in a dream. He still sees the house and surroundings as they were in his day, but at the same time he is aware of people and objects of the present day, like two pictures, one superimposed over the other. No wonder he doesn't know what is happening to him! Matthew seems like a ghost to him, intruding into this dream world and disturbing his thoughts, making him uncomfortably aware of what he knows at some deep level but does not wish to acknowledge – that he is dead, and should not be still clinging to his earthly home. But he cannot move on because, not knowing that there are other levels of the spiritual world, he has nowhere to go.

Souls of a similar mentality are drawn together in the after-death world. If they know no better, they live in a sort of collective dream, imagining that they are still on earth. Possibly Webbe's friends who wrote their names on the walls of Matthew's house were his companions in this existence.

Towards the end of the book, Matthew describes how he meets Webbe face to face, looking as real as a physical being. Matthew put out his hand to him – he must be one of the few people to have shaken hands with a ghost – and found himself grasping empty air. After that meeting, Webbe's presence became fainter until it faded away. One must hope that he found his way to a happier state of existence.

The most common cause of a soul becoming earthbound is violent death. The shock of the sudden separation from the body throws the soul into a state of turmoil. Like a person on earth who is in a state of shock or trauma following an accident, they relive the events of their death over and over in their minds like a nightmare.

In most cases where a person has died violently, the sense of shock soon passes. The soul will be met by someone, usually a relative, who helps them to recover and to adjust to being in the spirit world. Indeed, often there is no suffering and no awareness of the actual moment of death, but a few souls do become trapped in the places where they died. This may be, as I have said before, because of their inability to accept a spiritual state of existence. Alternatively, it may be the severity of the shock that holds them there; fear, anger, or, in the case of someone who was killed, a desire for vengeance on the murderer.

Souls who get caught up in this earthbound state are not suffering because of anything they did wrong on earth. It is true that a person of a spiritual disposition (not necessarily a conventionally religious person) or someone who had some knowledge of life after death, would be unlikely to get trapped, since they would quickly realize what had happened and would soon move onto a higher spiritual level. But it is not a question of morality. In ghost stories it is always the victim that haunts the scene of death, not the perpetrator of the crime, and this is so in reality. The spirit world is governed by thought so that the victim's own thoughts – and their ignorance of spiritual conditions – hold them imprisoned. This may not seem very fair, but then life isn't fair, and death does not automatically put right all injustices.

Places where there has been a concentration of violent emotion, such as battlefields, prisons and scenes of natural disasters become 'black spots,' vortices of negative energy. Souls who are lost can get sucked into these and find it hard to escape. A sensitive person visiting such a site will pick up a variety of impressions. There will be the memories impressed into the atmosphere, creating ghosts like the ghosts of the Roman legions described earlier, but there may also be some earthbound spirits there in need of rescue.

A few years ago I went on a coach trip to France. On the way back we passed through one of the First World War battlefields. When I got back home I felt tired and depressed and couldn't understand why. I had enjoyed the holiday and had no reason to be unhappy.

This went on for a couple of days, then gradually I became aware that it was not my own unhappiness I was feeling but that I was picking up the emotion from some spirit entity around me. I concentrated, and was aware of two young soldiers in First World War uniform. I knew they must have attached themselves to me as I passed through the place where they died because they sensed I would be able to help them. Without being conscious of what they were doing, they had travelled with me all the way back to England.

As I spoke to them and tried to explain the condition they were in, I was aware of another soldier, whom I took to be their commanding officer, who had come to help them. He told them to go with him. As they went to obey, one of the young soldiers – he could have been no more than sixteen – turned back to me and said, 'We're going back for the others.'

With that, they faded away. I had a mental picture of them passing out of their spiritual no man's land into light. I am sure that they did indeed go back to help any of their former companions that they could reach. One of the most satisfying things about doing this work is to know that, when one spirit is rescued, they in turn will rescue others.

I came across another example of this sort of 'black spot' when I was called to investigate an off-licence where the manager and his assistant had been experiencing disturbances; bottles were rattling on the shelves and the sound of heavy footsteps was heard from the flat above the shop. One member of staff who had left a heap of empty boxes in a corner of the cellar found them a little while later stacked up in a neat pile. At that point they considered taking the ghost onto the payroll! Ignoring the inevitable comments about spirits in bottles, I went along to see what I could find out.

As I sat in the flat, I was aware of the spirit of a boy who had been killed in the war. I could sense the sound of explosions and felt fire all around me. I felt that he had died abroad but that he had made his way back to the shop (which was a private house then) because his grandmother had lived there, and he had always gone to her when he was in trouble. He had not found her, however, or perhaps he had found her but she had been unaware of him. At any event, he was still trapped in the house.

I talked to him and explained to him that he did not need to stay there, that he should go with my spirit helpers who would take him to his grandmother. He left; but the disturbances continued. Obviously there was more to the case than I had realized. Then a friend who has lived in the area for many years told me that, during the war, a bomb had hit a cinema directly opposite the shop, killing many people. That accounted for the sensation of an explosion I had picked up. It also indicated to me that there might be other souls still trapped in the vicinity.

I enlisted the help of some friends who are mediums and together we concentrated on sending light into the shop and the surrounding area, to clear the negative vibrations and assist any souls who had died there and were still caught. This was successful. After a few days everything went quiet and since then there has been no more trouble.

Spirit entities are seldom able to affect physical matter, although they can make their presence felt mentally, but sometimes they do become violent, throwing things around and producing all manner of weird manifestations. These ghosts are called poltergeists, from the German meaning 'noisy spirit'.

As poltergeists often occur in houses where there are teenage children, parapsychologists tend to assume that the children are responsible. Some sort of telekenetic energy is produced by children at the age of puberty, particularly if they are unhappy or under stress and this, so the theory goes, is the cause of the trouble.

Mediums, however, claim that there is nearly always a spirit present in these cases, which uses the energy of the children, or anyone else who happens to be psychic. One researcher who supports this view is Guy Lyon Playfair. He describes a poltergeist as a kind of 'football of energy' which is kicked around by the spirits responsible, like schoolboys playing with a ball.

The former president of Wimbledon Spiritualist Church, a

medium called Bill Marie, was once called to investigate a case of poltergeist activity. The scene of the haunting was an unlikely one; a shed on an allotment, where seeds, plants and gardening equipment were kept. A number of people had reported violent activity there, with heavy objects being thrown around.

'It's been very active these last few days,' the owner of the shed told him when he arrived, accompanied by his friend Derek Robinson. They went inside, and immediately things started falling off the shelves and handfuls of seeds and grain were thrown in their faces, apparently out of mid-air.

Derek took one look and beat a hasty retreat. Bill wasn't far behind him. They stood outside listening. It sounded as if a fight was going on in the shed. Derek walked round cautiously to make sure that no one was playing tricks on them, which would have been difficult as it was broad daylight. Then Bill plucked up courage to go back in again by himself. As soon as he entered, all the noise ceased.

Bill and Derek visited the shed several times. Each time they were bombarded with flying objects. On one occasion a 56 lb weight went flying through the air, but neither of them was ever hit. Once a cross appeared written in the dust on the wall.

Bill eventually succeeded in contacting the haunting spirit and uncovered a sad story. The spirit was that of a boy of about twelve. He and his mother had lived in London but, when the Plague broke out, they had run away to the village of Bromley, as it then was. The villagers, however, had found out that they came from London and, fearing that they had brought the dreaded disease with them, had stoned them to death. The mother had been buried in unconsecrated ground, and because this troubled her, she could not be at peace. The poltergeist activity had been the boy's way of attracting attention to their plight.

Bill had prayers said for the mother. To show his gratitude, the boy promised that he would visit Bill's church. Bill and Derek returned to Wimbledon Church, wondering if he would keep his promise. As they went in, the inner doors opened and closed by themselves. After that, there were no more disturbances at the shed.

One of the most thoroughly investigated poltergeist cases of recent years, in a house in North London, displayed all the typical poltergeist features with a few particularly nasty variations of its own.

The Enfield poltergeist case began in 1977 and was investigated by Guy Lyon Playfair and Maurice Grosse of the Society for Psychical Research. It is described at length in Playfair's book *This House is Haunted.* The phenomena seemed to centre round Janet, one of the daughters of the family, who was twelve. Loud knocking sounds were heard, heavy furniture was moved, objects were hurled around the room, pools of water appeared on the floor, fires broke out, and electrical equipment brought in by the investigators inexplicably failed to work.

Playfair and Grosse recorded and witnessed literally hundreds of incidents, some of which took place before other witnesses, including policemen, journalists and TV crews. A woman police officer described in her report how a chair slid some three or four feet across the floor towards her. A reporter from the *Daily Mirror* told how he saw lego bricks, marbles and other objects flying around the house. One of the bricks struck him on the forehead, giving him a lump that lasted for several days.

The poltergeist directed most of its malice towards Janet, who complained of being kicked and pinched. She was frequently thrown out of bed and slung across the room. More than once it tried to strangle her with the curtains of the cord of her dressing-gown and she became subject to fits and violent trances.

Then the poltergeist began to speak. It spoke in a gruff, male voice which came from Janet's lips. Its conversation was limited mainly to obscenities but it claimed various identities, including Gober the Ghost and a number of former residents of the house. When asked where they came from, it replied, 'From the graveyard.'

Playfair enlisted the help of several mediums. Between them they contacted several different entities who they claimed were responsible for the haunting. Some were pathetic, lost souls, but others were more sinister. The medium Rose Gladden told Playfair: 'There's a lot of evil coming back to the earth right now. The ones behind it are the really bad ones, demons or whatever we want to call them.'

Which brings us to the question of evil spirits – do they exist? I have to say that, in twenty years as a medium, I have never come across what I would term an evil spirit although I have encountered many who, as in the examples I have given, are lost and in need of help. However, that is not to say that they don't exist. There are evil people in this world and, as we don't immediately change in character when we die, it is logical to assume that there are evil people on the other side of life also.

One medium who has experienced the darker aspect of the spirit world is Terry O'Sullivan. Terry describes himself as an exorcist, although he does not go to work armed with bell, book and candle. He sees exorcism or deliverance, as he prefers to call it, as a type of healing. In common with other mediums working in this field, he says that the vast majority of spirit entities that he is called upon to deal with are harmless – but there are exceptions, and this is where exorcism is needed.

He warns that anyone who deliberately seeks to contact the forces of darkness for personal gain, as in the use of black magic rites, is laying themselves open to attack by evil spirits or even by non-human entities he describes as demons. I asked him what was the worst case with which he had ever had to deal, and he told me a story that had all the ingredients of a classic black magic tale – and took place in the unlikely setting of Clacton-on-Sea.

He was called in by two sisters who were being terrorized by an entity haunting their house. Loud cracks and bangs had been heard, obscene words had been scribbled in lipstick on the dressing-table mirror and scratch marks had appeared on the woodwork which looked as though they had been made by claws. Terry traced the source of the trouble to the deceased husband of one of the sisters. He was told that, seven years before the man had died, he had become involved with a black magic group. His fortunes had taken an upward turn and he had made a lot of money. One day he was found dead on some waste ground, a look of terror on his face. The inquest returned an open verdict. After his death, his widow and her sister had a run of bad luck, and then the haunting began. On visiting the bungalow, Terry was at once aware of an evil force.

'It was a spirit with long hair and horns. I can only describe it as a satyr, as in Greek mythology. This creature attacked me, causing me severe pain. It entered my aura and held onto my spine. It was trying to gain control of my nervous system. If it had succeeded, I would have been taken over completely.'

A battle of wills ensued. At last, with the help of his protecting spirits whom he calls his guardians, Terry was able to fight off the attack and the satyr was despatched, but he was left in a state of exhaustion from which it took him three days to recover.

Terry has also been called to assist in cases of possession. One of his clients had been diagnosed schizophrenic because he had been taken over by an alien spirit. Terry was able to dislodge the entity, after which the patient returned to normal. According to Terry, some patients who are considered by doctors to be psychotic or schizophrenic are in fact suffering from possession, though he is not, of course, claiming that this is so in every instance.

Horror stories about evil spirits and possessions make some people question whether it is wise to seek contact with the spirit world at all. This is rather like saying that you should never cross the road because there is the possibility that you might get knocked down by a car. The spirit world is all around us whether we like it or not, so we might as well try to understand it. As I have already said, evil spirits are very rare and possession is rarer still, and there is no danger at all if you go about things in the right way. Motive is all important. If you seek with love and sincerity, you will draw to you only good.

However, the invisible world should never be treated lightly and there are dangers in dabbling in the unknown out of idle curiosity. For this reason, Terry is very much opposed to the use of ouija boards. These devices are, as he says, 'like open doors into the spirit world.' Used by experienced and spiritually minded people they may give interesting results, but they are a greater potential danger to those who play around with them not knowing what they are doing. They may attract lost or even harmful spirits who are then hard to get rid of.

Terry believes that the work of rescuing lost souls is very necessary and that more mediums are needed to do it. However, special qualities are required.

'You need to be strong to do this work. People who are emotional or highly strung should leave it well alone. You must have great faith and not be afraid of the darkness. And, above all, you must love God.'

Those who become skilled in this task are, he believes, 'pioneers who help us all to the greater understanding of the many different levels of the inner worlds.'

So what should you do if you have a problem in your home with things that go bump in the night? First of all, look for a natural explanation; draughts from windows, creaking floorboards and the like. If you still feel there is a presence there, call in a medium. A priest may be able to help by blessing the house or performing a service of exorcism, but most priests have little understanding of the spirit world and a medium should be able to contact the spirit and help them rather than simply trying to drive them away.

You can assist yourself, by talking to the spirit and sending out kind thoughts and prayers but, in view of what has been said above, don't attempt to contact them using an ouija board or any other device of the kind.

Most of all, don't be frightened. It is highly unlikely that there is anything nasty there. In all probability it is only a poor, lost soul who deserves your pity. Imagine how you would feel if you were desperately seeking help and couldn't make anyone hear, and try to help them. After all, we are all going to be ghosts one day.

8 'So This is Death …'

There are two things you can do about death. You can shut your mind to it, pretending it is something that only happens to other people, or you can look it squarely in the face and try to discover what, if anything, lies beyond it. The second alternative seems to me the more sensible. However much we would like to think that we are immortal, we know that we will all one day reach the final curtain and, even before this happens, the chances are that we will have to suffer, at least once in our lives, the death of someone we love. So we may as well confront our fears now – and perhaps we'll find that they are not so terrible after all.

I have had one close encounter with death, and it was an experience I shall never forget. I was nineteen at the time and had contracted jaundice which threatened to develop into meningitis. I had been ill for about three weeks. One night, my temperature soared. I was weak and feverish and felt myself drifting in and out of consciousness. Waves of faintness came over me, each one a little stronger than the last. It was like being swept out by the tide. 'This is it,' I thought. 'I'm dying!'

I had never been afraid of death before. All my life I had had an instinctive awareness that death wasn't the end. After my grandmother's death, some years before, I had felt her presence around me and I believed that she would be there to meet me. But believing is one thing and being confronted with the reality is something entirely different. I called upon God, though I had never been much of one for saying my prayers, and begged him desperately to let me live.

Then suddenly a great calm descended on me. I seemed to be floating through a velvety blackness. I felt warm and protected. All fear vanished. It no longer mattered to me whether I lived or died. Either way, I knew I would be safe and I was content to resign myself to whatever happened.

I don't know how long the feeling lasted. It could have been a couple of minutes, it could have been hours; I was suspended in timelessness. But it faded into a natural sleep. When I woke my temperature was back to normal and, from that time on, I began to get better.

The same calm and feeling of peace that I found so comforting is often experienced by the dying. We go through our lives fearing death, yet when the end actually comes, fear vanishes. This fact has often been noticed by doctors and nurses and those who attend the dying. Frequently they report that a change comes over patients in the last days or hours of their lives. They become mentally withdrawn, as if preparing themselves to depart. They accept what is happening and their mood changes to contentment, resignation, even exhilaration. This is so even in those who profess no belief in an afterlife. It is as though they have some unconscious inner knowledge that they stand on the threshold of a new existence.

During their closing days, dying people often speak of seeing friends and relatives who have died before coming to meet them. This is not hallucination; it occurs in patients who are sound and clear in their minds and have never before had any psychic experiences. Interestingly, they hardly ever report seeing visions of people who are still alive.

The founder of the Society for Psychical Research, Sir William Barrett, published in 1926 a study of death-bed visions. He noted particularly incidents where the dying person reported seeing the spirit form of someone of whose death they had not been told. One of the accounts quoted was provided by his wife, who was a gynaecologist. Lady Barrett was called urgently to a dying patient:

When I entered the ward Mrs B. held out her hands to me and said, 'Thank you, thank for what you have done for me – for bringing the baby. Is it a boy or girl?' Then holding my hand tightly she said, 'Don't leave me, don't go away, will you?' And after a few minutes, while the House Surgeon carried out some restorative measures, she lay looking up towards the open part of the room, which was brightly lighted, and said, 'Oh, don't let it get dark – it's getting so dark ... darker and darker.' Her husband and mother were sent for.

Suddenly she looked eagerly towards one part of the room, a

radiant smile illuminating her whole countenance. 'Oh, lovely, lovely,' she said. I asked, 'What is lovely?' 'What I *see*,' she replied in low, intense tones. 'What do you see?' 'Lovely brightness – wonderful beings.' It is difficult to describe the sense of reality conveyed by her intense absorption in the vision.

Then – seeming to focus her attention more intently on one place for a moment – she exclaimed, almost with a kind of joyous cry, 'Why, it's Father! Oh, he's so glad I'm coming; he *is* so glad. It would be perfect if only W. (her husband) could come too.'

Her baby was brought for her to see. She looked at it with interest, and then said, 'Do you think I ought to stay for baby's sake?' Then turning towards the vision again, she said, 'I can't – I can't stay; if you could see what I do, you would know I can't stay.'

But she turned to her husband, who had come in, and said, 'You won't let baby go to anyone who won't love him, will you?' Then she gently pushed him to one side, saying, 'Let me see the lovely brightness.'[1]

The matron of the hospital confirmed Lady Barrett's account. She added that the patient had also spoken of seeing her sister. This sister had died three weeks before but, because of the patient's serious illness, the news had been kept from her.

A similarly moving story was told to me by an elderly lady, Dolly, who was in hospital for an operation. In the bed next to hers was a sixteen-year-old girl who had had a burst appendix:

She said she could see her mother, who had died a few years before, and Jimmy, her brother. Her eyes would light up and she would sit up in bed and talk to them. Just before she died, she said, 'Look at all the lights! Move over, Jimmy, so that I can see. I've only got four more steps to go.' Then she held out her arms and called, 'Mother!' and that was the last word she spoke.

The experience of death is often worse for the family and friends, who have to stand helplessly by, than for the dying person themself. It is hard to let go of someone you love, but if you can accept that they are not ceasing to be but merely moving onto another stage of existence, then it is easier to let them go with dignity, instead of trying to hold them back in a body which may be causing them pain.

Healing is of great benefit at this time, but it should be seen as a way of assisting the person to pass over peacefully, rather than as a desperate last-ditch attempt to prolong life. If you send out healing prayers for someone who is dying, simply pray that they may be helped in whatever way is best for them. These prayers will make their transition easier and help them to adjust more quickly when they reach the other side of life.

A friend of mine who is a medium told me how she coped with the death of her husband following a heart attack.

> He was rushed into intensive care. I went with him and sat by the bed. I didn't know which way it was going to go. As he wasn't all that old, the doctors said there was a chance he might pull through. I prayed for him and asked for healing. As I did so, I saw an immense light. It was shining through the curtains that had been drawn around the bed. I spoke to him in my mind and said, 'Whatever is meant to be, go with it. Go with the light.' Sadly – for me, at least – he had a second heart attack shortly afterwards and died. But when I looked at him, there was a smile on his face and I felt a great peace.

A few days later, in a message from another medium, he told her, 'The prayers at the hospital opened a door for me. I was able to go into the light.'

So death can be seen as a release. When we die we simply cast off the physical body like an outworn suit or clothing for which we have no further use. And perhaps this would be a good point to explain about the various bodies of which we are composed.

We are apt to identify with our physical bodies, to say that we 'are' a body and 'have' a soul, but it would be more true to say that we 'are' a soul, which is contained within several bodies or sheaths. These bodies interpenetrate, one inside the other, like Russian dolls. Each one is composed of a finer material and vibrates at a higher rate than the one before.

The physical body, our outer casing, is the most dense. After this comes the etheric. The etheric can be seen by clairvoyants in the aura as a band of greyish-white light that extends half an inch or so around the physical form. While we are alive, it is literally what holds body and soul together. It forms the connecting link between the two, feeding the physical with the vital life energy or prana it needs to keep itself alive.

Every night when we go to sleep the etheric moves out of the physical. For this reason, sleep has been called a little death.

Studies of out of the body experiences have provided us with detailed information as to what the etheric body is like. It is a replica of the physical but composed of a finer material. It is weightless and can move at great speed, propelled by the power of thought. It is free of the imperfections of the physical – for instance, a person who had had a limb amputated would still have that limb in their etheric form – but it does not suffer pain or weakness.

The etheric body is always attached to the physical by a cord. This is referred to in the Bible: 'or ever the Silver Cord be loosed, the golden bowl broken ... then shall the dust return to the earth and the spirit shall return unto God who gave it.' The cord can be extended to infinite length but it is never broken until we die. Then, like an umbilical cord, it is severed, setting the soul free.

Clairvoyants who have been present at the moment of death have witnessed this process. They have described seeing a cloud or column of vapour detach itself from the physical body and rise above it. For a few moments it hovers, suspended above the physical form, the cord still attached. Then it moves into an upright position, the cord snaps, and the spirit body moves away free. After a short period – usually about three days – the etheric body dissolves and thereafter the soul dwells in the astral, or spirit body, which will be described in more detail in the next chapter.

Of recent years there has been much study of the 'near death experience', the accounts of those who have been clinically dead but have been resuscitated by doctors. The first person to bring this research to the attention of the public was an American doctor, Raymond Moody. His book *Life After Life.* published in 1975, became a bestseller. Following his work, other doctors and psychiatrists, notably Elisabeth Kübler-Ross and Kenneth Ring in America and Margot Grey in this country, began questioning their patients and their findings confirmed Moody's. An enormous amount of material has now been collected from people of different nationalities and cultures, religious believers and atheists, even from young children. Taken as a whole it displays a remarkable consistency. If we consider these NDE accounts in conjunction with the accounts received through mediums from those who have crossed the barrier of death and not returned, we can build up a clear picture of what it is like to die.

A very typical near death experience was recounted to me by a lady called Jill. She was twenty-six when it happened and had read none of the literature on the subject.

> I had a bad bout of flu for which I was given antibiotics. After the second dose I started to feel unwell. I said, 'I'm going to pass out.'
>
> I didn't lose consciousness. I heard a whirring or buzzing sound. I felt as if I was being pulled upwards. I remember thinking, I must be coming round. I opened my eyes, as I thought, but everything around me was dark. I couldn't understand why I was seeing darkness when my eyes were open. I felt slightly strange but warm, elated and happy. I thought, so this is death … but I'm not dead. It's wonderful! Death must be another kind of life. I was so taken up with this that I was beginning to lose my memory of what was happening on earth. Everything was retreating. Although it was still dark there was a glistening around me.
>
> Then I heard a bang and heard Chris (her husband) calling my name. I could see him as if I was looking through the wrong end of a telescope. He was bending over me on the kitchen floor, shaking me. He was very distressed. I realized I was looking down on him from ceiling height. The bang had been him opening the window to get more air into the room.
>
> I suddenly thought, how is he going to cope with bringing up two young children on his own? And as I thought this, the whole process went into reverse. I heard the buzzing again then I came back into my body in the same way as I had gone out. But I didn't want to come back; it was the thought of my children that made me return. Ever since then, I've felt that there was a purpose to my life. If this is death, then I won't be afraid to die.

Doris Stokes also had a close brush with death, as she recounts in her book, *Voices in my Ear*:

> I opened my eyes slightly and the bed was surrounded by a beautiful turquoise light. Blue light I vaguely remembered, the healing power. I looked again and my father and son John Michael (who passed over when he was a baby) were standing at the foot of the bed. They were smiling at me and I tried to smile back. If I'm going to die, I thought, all I have to do is to go to them. Then the blue light started spinning and other colours whirled into it and I felt myself drawn feet first into a brilliant rainbow spiral. I was rushing down, my father and John Michael a little ahead of me, and beyond them at the end of that tunnel of madly flashing colours was a bright light so bright I couldn't look

at it. Instinctively I knew that if I reached the light I would have passed over. Yet the only emotion I felt was relief. I don't have to fight any more I thought, it's out of my hands.

Suddenly there was a tremendous jolt and I crashed back to the bed again. The tunnel, my father and John Michael were gone ...

... I nearly died but strange as it may sound, I'm not sorry. I knew there was nothing to fear ...

Though the near death experience is different for everyone who undergoes it, there are certain features which have been found to occur again and again, and these have become known as the 'core experience'. The sequence of events begins with the separation from the body. There is a sense of euphoria, of being surrounded by love and peace. Some people have spoken of hearing beautiful music. Then comes the entry into darkness, described as a sensation of travelling at great speed down a long, dark tunnel. This is followed by meetings with deceased friends and relatives or an encounter with a Christ-like figure or being of light. Then comes the life review, in which the person sees the whole of their life in flashback. Finally, they come to a barrier which they cannot pass or else they are told by someone that they must return to the body. They do so with great reluctance, but come back with a changed outlook on life. They have a greater sense of purpose and a heightened compassion for others. Most significantly, they have lost their fear of death.

All these features can be found in the accounts of those who have died. Helen Salter, speaking through the medium Geraldine Cummins describes to her husband the moment of her death:

My turn to make what some believe is a long journey. But for me it was such a short journey. Oh, it was so incredibly easy and painless. There was only very brief nightmare, when I wanted to get back into my body in order to return to you. An instant's bad dream. That's all death was to me. After it, almost immediately, there came the unimaginable moment – a welcoming mother and father ... In the past we, you and I, have wondered what our arrival to this level would be like. But nothing we supposed came up to that beautiful, surprising, homely feeling I had with these two protectors waiting for me ... Death's exit is so simple, and all our lives we have made it so complicated ...[2]

A man who in life had been a Christian scientist explains how he died:

> I had been standing talking to my gardener. Then I found myself still talking to him, but he didn't appear to hear me. I noticed he seemed in a great state of agitation and then went down on his knees. I looked down and saw him kneeling beside what appeared to be me. I couldn't make out at first what had happened. Then he hurried away to get help.
>
> I was under the impression that I must be dreaming. It was so strange to be standing there looking at what was apparently myself lying on the ground. Gradually this scene faded and I found myself in quite another place. I was surprised and delighted to see my mother holding out her arms to me, and beside her my brother, C.D. Then it began to dawn on me that I had passed on. Since then, I have had a lot to learn. I can now understand a great deal that seemed difficult to explain before. I feel sure that if people were to know that the actual moment of passing is not even noticeable, the fear of death that haunts so many people would vanish. It is largely the fear of the unknown. If more was known about this after-life, that fear would cease to a great extent.[3]

Mary Lodge, the widow of Sir Oliver Lodge, tells of hearing music and meeting her mother and children:

> The first clear recollection I had after my mortal eyes watched the anxious looks of my dear husband and children, was being borne upward by heavenly sweet music of welcome, and when the last song died away I felt myself being placed on a soft downy couch of flowers and carried into a white temple. I have since leared that it is called the Temple of Repose.
>
> I awoke in the arms of our living mother and our own dear children who had made the heavenly journey before me, and oh! the joy of the meeting! After a little lady came to us, all in white, and said, 'All is ready,' and then our mother told me that we would proceed to the Temple of Prayer. We then marched in a procession, I walking by the side of our noble son. We passed through beautiful gardens and groves and beautiful fringed walls entwined with lovely snow-white lilies. Then we came to an arch of white glittering stone, pure as crystal, and in letters of gold written across it were these words: IN THIS LAND THERE IS NO DEATH.[4]

Doris Stokes recounts the sensation of travelling down a tunnel, and the process of transition is sometimes described in similar terms. A young man who was killed in a plane crash said,

> I saw in front of me a dark tunnel. I stepped out of the tunnel into a new world.[5]

The 'Being of Light' is mentioned in many communications. It is described sometimes as Jesus or Christ, sometimes as a guide or a teacher from a higher plane. A young woman, Patricia, speaking to her mother on earth calls it simply 'the Presence':

> It's not in the least like the idea of Presence that I had connected with God, something awe-inspring that would make you hold your breath in wonder, and feel smaller than nothing – here was something exactly the reverse. It literally pours into you, making you want to laugh and be gay, something that nestles closer than oneself to oneself – closer even than Johnny [her husband] and yet it seems to be Johnny, or that Johnny is part of *it*. There is a feeling of breathing the same Divinity.[6]

Another common feature is the life review. This is often very rapid and is reminiscent of the superstition that a dying man sees the whole of his past life flash before his eyes. T.E. Lawrence (Lawrence of Arabia) who was killed in a motorcycle accident, recounted:

> A ribbon of road, boys on bicycles, my cottage, and soon these discreet memories began to coalesce into a continuous series of past experiences. Before long I was racing back along the years faster and faster, helpless to stay the record and obliged to feel as well as to remember as my past unrolled back to the earliest childhood memories.[7]

There is an element of self-judgement in this kaleidoscope of memories, of seeing oneself as one truly is – and perhaps finding the experience a humbling one. But it would appear that this is just a preliminary review. When the soul has had time to adjust there comes a deeper and more penetrating self-analysis; but that belongs to a later stage.

Death is easiest for those who slip away quietly, having come to the natural end of their earthly existence. Someone they know, usually a close relative, will come to meet them and lead them away. But those who die suddenly, like the Christian scientist mentioned earlier, are often confused and don't realize what has happened to them. A farmer called Hopkins gave this account at a Leslie Flint séance.

> I just had a stroke, or seizure, or heart attack. Or something of that sort. As a matter of fact I was harvesting. I felt a bit peculiar, thought it was the sun and went down in the 'edge. I felt a bit drowsy, a bit peculiar, and must have dozed off. But dear, oh dear, I had such a shock.
>
> I woke up, as I thought. The sun had gone down. And there was me, or what appeared to be me. I couldn't make head nor tail of it. It never struck me at all that I was dead.[8]

Hopkins walked along the road to the doctor's. On the way he passed some of his old cronies, who just walked through him. At the doctor's he heard people talking about him and saying that he was dead, then he saw them taking his body to the chapel. Still confused, he went to the vicarage thinking that the vicar would be able to explain things to him but found that he couldn't see him either. He was eventually met by his wife, who took him to his home in the astral world.

Farmer Hopkins' period of confusion was comparatively brief but some souls have a much harder time coming to terms with their passing, particularly if they died in traumatic circumstances. Stephen Turoff, the psychic surgeon, has written a book which was dictated to him by a soldier called Legget who died in the Battle of the Somme. Legget was hit by a piece of shell and lay for hours in agony before he passed out.

> When I recovered I felt dazed but experienced little pain and no longer felt weak and tired. I put my hand to my chest to determine how much damage had been done by the shrapnel. To my amazement there was not a tear in my tunic. I hauled myself up with great difficulty because I was in complete darkness. Although they sounded distant, I heard the guns and clamour around me. After a while I became used to the darkness, which resembled a thick mist, and saw amidst it dark shadows flitting to and fro. Other shadows lay still. I decided to move on; I didn't want to get caught or to be cut off from the rest of the lads.[9]

Legget saw two people coming towards him. They bent over the shadowy heap on the ground which, to his amazement, he realized was his own body. 'He's gone, poor fellow,' he heard one of them say. 'Put him round the back with the rest for burial.'

> The voices faded into the mist and I heard no more. I slowly ran my hands over my body and face. I still had a body, but yet they must have buried something. By now the realization that I might actually be dead slowly began to dawn on me. I was terribly confused and afraid. I wondered what on earth would happen next. If I were dead, where was heaven? I began to cry uncontrollably and uttered, 'Dear God, please help me. I know I never went to church, but I always tried to be good.'
>
> I looked about myself and gazed across to where the cries of war were coming from. I could see many shapes running, falling. Some got up, others just lay there. I noted one in particular. As I watched, I saw a fine mist pour out of it and mould itself into the figure of a man who hovered above the dark shape. With astonishment, I assumed this must have happened to me. The man began to stir and struggle. Obviously he was unable to understand what was happening, much as I had been. I thought, 'Poor sod, perhaps I can at least help him in some way or other.'
>
> It didn't take long to reach him. As I approached, I heard his crying as he struggled. I shouted. 'Don't panic! I'll help you.' At the same time I was thinking. 'God knows how as you're much bigger than me.' He saw me and began to scream, 'Help me, mate, what's happened to me?' 'Well,' I said, 'I think we're dead.'
>
> 'Don't be a daft bastard,' he shouted. 'How can I be? I'm talking to you! How can I be dead? Everyone knows that when you're dead, you're dead.'

The two men wandered about in a mist for some time, then they saw a light coming towards them. Out of the light emerged one of their former officers who led them and other dead soldiers away from the battlefield and, gradually, they learned to adjust to their new state. Had this not happened they might have become earthbound and continued to haunt the scene of the battle.

Even when the manner of death is violent, the dying person is rarely aware of the actual moment when death takes place. Mike Swain, a young man who was killed in a car accident, felt nothing of the impact:

The sun is glaring on the windscreen of the black car, and reflecting back into my eyes. I can see nothing but a bright silver radiance. It is blinding me. All of a sudden, the radiance changes from silver to gold, I am being lifted up in the air, out through the top of the car ...[10]

Mike tells his mother, 'Never allow yourself to mourn. When you do, it vitally depresses me in this world.' This plea is frequently made by those who communicate. Of course grieving is natural and needs to be expressed, and there is bound to be a period of mourning following the death of a loved one. But excessive and prolonged grieving holds a soul back. They are aware of our thoughts and are bound to feel distressed if those they love are unhappy. It is a good thing, when a person dies, to allow them to make contact through a medium if they wish to do so, since this comforts them as much as it comforts those left behind, but we shouldn't cling to them when the period of mourning is over. It is a mistake to be ever seeking for 'messages' or asking their advice about trivial things we ought to decide for ourselves. While we still think of them and remember them with affection a mental link always remains, like a telephone line. We can call them if we need them and they will in any case be aware of what is happening in our lives and be around from time to time, especially when we are going through periods of difficulty. But life has to go on, for us and for them.

Dying is rather like going to live in another country. Someone who has emigrated will probably ring the family up as soon as they arrive, to let them know they have got there safely and tell them what the place is like. After that, they will phone sometimes or occasionally return to visit. But they cannot settle down properly if they are always being pestered by their relatives ringing them up, sobbing and wanting them to come back home.

The best thing we can do for someone who has died is to send out our loving thoughts and prayers and wish them God speed on their journey. This will aid them to find their feet quickly and, when they do return, it will not be with sad memories but with happiness and renewed vigour, and a greater love for us than it was possible for them to feel while on earth.

Our whole attitude to death needs changing. It should be regarded not as an end but as a step forward; a part of the natural cycle of existence. The spirit teacher Silver Birch has this to say to those who are bereaved:

> Think of the miracle of the seasons, the eternal circle forever revolving with unbroken constancy – the snows of winter, when all life sleeps; the herald of spring, when life awakens; the fulness of summer, when life is revealed in all its beauty; autumn, when the voice of nature is hushed and preparation is made for sleep ere the period of refreshment comes upon it.
>
> The cycle is repeated in every human life. the pageant of nature is duplicated in every human soul. First there is the spring, with the awakening consciousness; the summer, when man's powers rise to their highest; autumn, when life begins to wane; and winter, when sleep comes to the weary, tired soul.
>
> But even after the winter of the physical life, spring comes to the spirit as it awakens in another world to continue that eternal cycle. Take from nature this message, and be assured that the laws which have never failed will continue to operate in your case and in the case of every human life.[11]

And what is it like, this world that awaits us? Those who have had near death experiences have described it as a very beautiful place. The following account is typical:

> At some point I suddenly found myself in this beautiful place. I was greeted by such warmth and happiness that it was utter bliss. I was in a beautiful landscape, the flowers, trees, the colours were indescribable, not at all like the colours you see here. The peace and joy were overpowering, I felt warm and glowing. There was a blinding light, but it was not harsh and did not hurt my eyes. The beauty of the landscape is beyond description. Somewhere I heard the most wonderful music and there was an organ playing as well. I felt embraced by such love, it's beyond description.[12]

Obviously, these people who have been brought back to life can have no more than a tantalizing glimpse of what lies beyond. But, if we compare their accounts with those received from the dead themselves, we find that they correspond closely. By weighing up all the descriptions that have been received, it is possible for us to do what man in earlier ages could not. We can lift the veil on death and look into the country beyond.

9   Into the Spirit World

I cannot of course, speak from personal experience. I have not been there. However much we may speculate about what the spirit or astral world is like, we cannot really know until we get there ourselves – and by that time we are usually not in a position to tell anyone else about it. Those who do communicate from beyond the grave have difficulty in describing the place in which they have arrived. They are limited by the confines of language, which does not contain words subtle enough for what they want to convey, and by the ability of the medium to receive the strange concepts that they are trying to put across.

On the occasions when I have spoken to deceased friends and asked them, 'What is it like over there?' their replies have been vague. Even those who had thought they were well informed have admitted, 'It's not quite what I expected,' but when pressed to explain in what way it is different, they seem to be at a loss for words.

We do, however, have some information to go on. Numerous travellers have returned from beyond the bourn and recounted their adventures. In reading them, we must make allowances for the tendency of mediums, consciously or unconsciously, to colour the communications they receive. But the accounts are in the main consistent and have been so since modern mediumship began. The eighteenth century philosopher and seer, Emanuel Swedenborg, spoke of a world which sounded like an idealized version of this world:

> Lands appear there, mountains, hills, valleys, plains, fields, lakes, rivers, springs of water, as in the natural world; animals appear there, birds and fishes of every kind ... the universe of the spiritual world is thus quite similar to the universe of the natural world, with only this difference, that the things which are there

are not fixed and settled like those in the natural world, because
there is not anything natural there but all is spiritual.[1]

It is interesting to compare this with the NDE account given at
the end of the last chapter. Spiritualist literature is full of similar
descriptions of the land known as the 'Summerland,' of which
the following is a typical example:

> Already I was conscious of the revitalizing effect of this heavenly
> garden to such an extent that I was anxious to see more of it. And
> so, in company with my old friend, upon whom I was here relying
> for information and guidance, I walked the garden paths, trod
> upon the exquisite grass, whose resilience and softness were
> almost comparable to 'walking on air' and tried to make myself
> realize that all this superlative beauty was part of my own home.
>
> There were many splendid trees to be seen, none of which was
> malformed, such as one is accustomed to see on earth, yet there
> was no suggestion of strict uniformity of pattern. It was simply
> that each tree was growing under perfect conditions, free from
> the storms of wind that bend and twist the young branches, and
> free from the inroads of insect life and many other causes of the
> misshapenness of earthly trees. As with the flowers, so with the
> trees. They live for ever incorruptible, clothed always in their full
> array of leaves of every shade of green, and for ever pouring out
> life to all those who approach near them.
>
> I had observed that there did not appear to be what we should
> commonly call shade beneath the trees, and yet there did not
> appear to be any glaring sun. It seemed to be that there was a
> radiance of light that penetrated into every corner, and yet there
> was no hint of flatness. My friend told me that all light proceeded
> directly from the Giver of all light, and that this light was Divine
> life itself, and that it bathed and illumined the whole of the spirit
> world where lived those who had eyes spiritually to see.
>
> I noticed, too, that a comfortable warmth pervaded every inch
> of space, a warmth perfectly even and as perfectly sustained. The
> air had a stillness, yet there were gentle perfume-laden breezes –
> the truest zephyrs – that in no way altered the delightful
> balminess of the temperature.[2]

The people that live in these surroundings exist in perfect
contentment and harmony. It is all very beautiful – but a little
sickly. Some would say that it bears more than a passing
resemblance to Battersea Park on a warm August bank holiday,

with everyone lounging around enjoying themselves and being impossibly nice to everyone else. Family reunions also loom large in these descriptions, which is not necessarily an encouraging prospect; coming face to face with all those ghastly relatives you thought you'd seen the last of.

Some such region as the Summerland does seem to exist however. It is a spiritual counterpart of the earth that reflects its beauty and has none of its ugliness, and most people do find their way there, by which time, presumably, they have learned to take a more charitable attitude towards their relatives and the world in general. But this state is not heaven and we do not have to pass through the day of judgement to earn it.

For there is one very basic fact we have to grasp about death, and that is that all the traditional images that most of us had drummed into us as children are fundamentally mistaken. There are no pearly gates and no harps and, if there are angels, they are not wearing wings. Nor is there a hell of fire and brimstone to which sinners are condemned for ever. In fact, there is nothing final about death. It is just another step along the road to life.

The first surprise, as we begin to delve into these deceased travellers' tales, is how similar the next world seems to be to this one, but the similarity is deceptive. The spirit world is governed by its own laws and, until these are understood, much that we read about it will seem confusing, not to say wildly improbable.

The most important of these laws, and the hardest one for our earthly minds to grasp, is this: The spirit world is ruled by thought. Everything there is brought into being and maintained by the power of thought. As you think, so you are, and so you create your own conditions.

Let us examine this concept in more detail. In a way, the material world is illusionary. We think of matter as being solid but in fact we know that it is made up of atoms vibrating at a tremendous rate. But physicists are discovering, by analysing ever more and more minute particles of matter, that there is a point at which matter and energy become interchangeable. In other words, matter is energy solidified.

On the spirit or astral plane, which is, so to speak, the next rung up the ladder of evolution, matter exists, but it is of a finer, more rarified kind, able to be moulded by the power of thought.

We are all familiar these days with the idea that thoughts are powerful. Psychics like Uri Geller have demonstrated its ability to affect material things; spoon-bending is just one trivial example of this. Many books have been written on the power of the mind, explaining how, by the technique of creative visualization, it is possible to get almost anything you want, just by thinking about it and willing it. Imagine for a moment that this was a literal reality. You want a house in the country, you think about it and it appears. You want to visit a friend in a distant place so you concentrate your mind on them and, hey presto! you are there. The spirit world is a bit like that. Thoughts take on substance. What you wish for, you can create – but only within certain limits, as we shall see.

I have made it sound like a dream world, and indeed the astral has been called the 'Plane of Illusion'. But here we come up against the problem of language. Words are inadequate to convey this sort of reality. Dreams and illusions are shadowy things; yet to the dwellers on the astral plane, everything around them is as real and solid as everything on earth is to us.

We enter this world, as I have already explained, as soon as we shed the physical body. Of course, we leave behind our material possessions. There is a saying that 'you can't take it with you.' ('If I can't take it with me,' a wealthy old uncle of mine used to remark, 'then I'm not going!') But in fact, we do take a lot of things with us; our characters, our desires, our thoughts and memories. And these are what determines the kind of conditions – pleasant or unpleasant – we find ourselves in. By a natural law of attraction, we gravitate toward the level of spirit life for which we are most suited. This does not depend upon what religion we followed or what we believed; it depends upon the sort of person we were and the kind of life we lived.

The astral plane is vast and immensely varied and the Summerland is just part of it. To attempt to describe all the astral regions would require a book in itself, and even this is just one of the many planes that exist in the world beyond death. Traditionally, the universe has been depicted as consisting of seven planes, one above the other. At the bottom is the earth or physical plane. The astral plane lies above this and after the astral come various mental and higher spiritual realms, culminating in heaven at the very top of the pyramid.

Each plane is in turn sub-divided into seven sub-planes, at which point things start getting very complicated, so I will not attempt a more precise description. The image is, in any case, a little misleading. The planes are not geographical areas but could be more accurately described as dimensions or states of consciousness. There is no hard and fast division between one plane and another. They merge into each other like the colours on a printer's shade card.

Not only do they merge, they also interpenetrate, but because they are vibrating at different rates, they are able to occupy the same physical space independently of each other. The astral plane, being closest in its rate of vibration to the physical plane, can interact with it more easily than the others.

It is possible to shift from one level to another by making a change in consciousness. This is in fact what mediums do when they attune to spirit. The spirit world is always around us but we are usually unaware of it. One might use the analogy of radio waves; these are in the air all the time but we do not hear them unless we tune in with the appropriate instrument.

To die then, is simply to make a shift of consciousness from the physical to the astral level, which is why it is so easy and painless. But after the soul has finally freed itself of the body, what happens then? It is impossible to generalize about this question. We have already seen how the experience can vary from one individual to another, from Helen Salter's joyous reunion with her parents to Farmer Hopkins' confused wanderings among his unsuspecting colleagues. Each person's journey is different, depending on their temperament. Some immediately feel at home and adapt themselves quickly, others arrive unprepared and take a long while to find their astral feet.

But the average, decent-living man or woman has nothing to fear from death. So, by way of illustration, let us invent an imaginary character – we'll call him Adam Smith – and follow him as he sets out on the Supreme Adventure.

We'll suppose that he is a conventional man, honest and uncomplicated, with a kind disposition but not particularly religious. He dies in hospital at an advanced age, after a period of illness. Without being aware of what is happening, he slips out of the body and finds himself travelling down a long, dark tunnel.

He comes out of the end and finds himself standing beside himself, looking down at his body on the bed. At first he can't understand what has happened. He feels and looks just as he did a moment before, except that all his pain and weakness has gone. He is even dressed in his old familiar jacket and trousers. He tries to speak to his family but they don't hear. The doctors are saying he is dead, which seems ridiculous, as he is very much alive.

Before he has time to grasp the situation, he sees his mother coming towards him. She takes him by the hand, and suddenly the walls of the hospital seem to melt away. He feels himself floating upwards and comes to land in a place that seems strangely familiar.

It is for all the world as if he was still on earth and walking in the countryside he knew as a child. On either side is a gently undulating landscape. The trees and grass are a lush shade of green such as he has never seen before. Houses are dotted here and there. There is a gentle breeze blowing and the air is filled with the sound of bird song. The light is dazzling yet it does not hurt his eyes. All is peace and he feels himself enveloped in love.

His mother takes him to one of the houses. It is small but pretty, just the sort of place he dreamed of on earth but could never afford. His wife, who died some years before, is waiting at the door. He is filled with joy at the sight of her; his last years, after she died, were lonely. Both she and his mother are unchanged, except that they seem to have grown younger and are vibrantly alive. A young woman is standing beside his wife. Although he has never seen her before, he seems to recognize her. His wife tells him that this is their daughter, who died in infancy.

He is taken inside the house and shown round. It is decorated exactly to his taste. To his surprise, he finds many of the things he had in his earthly home, including his treasured books and pictures. Even his old dog is there. It bounds towards him, wagging his tail, and there is such intelligence in its eyes that it is almost as if it can speak.

His mother asks him if he would like a nice cup of tea, and produces a tea-tray, with home-made cakes just like the ones she used to bake. The food is as real and substantial as everything else around him. Too bemused by now to question, he eats and drinks, and feels refreshed. Then she suggests that he should rest for a while, and shows him to a bedroom where he lays down on the bed. As he falls into a slumber he reflects that all this seems like a dream – which, in a sense, is what it is.

* * *

This fictionalized account is typical of many that have been received. Cynics may sneer at their apparent absurdity. A rural English heaven of tea and cakes and thatched cottages with roses round the door! Perhaps God is, after all, an Englishman. But it is not as absurd as it first appears. Adam Smith has entered into a world of his own creation.

It has been said that we make our own heaven or hell while we are still on earth, and this is indeed the case. Our afterlife is built up of our thoughts, memories and desires. No wonder it seems familiar to us! Adam's idea of heaven was a little house in the country with his wife and family. That was what he thought about and longed for when he was on earth and, by thinking about it and longing for it, he has unconsciously created it, so when he dies he finds it there waiting for him.

He has not created it by his own unaided efforts. His family and those who share it with him have helped to build it. It is, you might say, a collective thought creation, shaped by all those who inhabit it.

Every place on earth has its astral equivalent. There are towns and cities as well as countryside. An inhabitant of say, the African jungle, would find himself still in the jungle, but in an idealized version of it, where there were no mosquitos and the animals did not hunt one another for food.

The knowledge that such paradise conditions exist is embedded deep in man's subconscious mind and is reflected in many different religions, under different names. In Spiritualism, which knows more about the after death state than any other religion, it is called the Summerland. To the North American Indians it was the Happy Hunting Ground. The ancient Egyptians looked forward to entering Amenti, and Land of the West. The Greeks had the Elysian Fields, and the Celts, the Isles of the Blessed. Viking warriors faced death fearlessly in the certainty that they would wake in Valhalla, where they could feast and drink to their hearts' content. No doubt they were not disappointed. As their thoughts had created their afterlife, so they would have found it.

But our Adam Smith is no warrior. His desires are simple and easily satisfied. Let us follow him as he awakes from his sleep and begins to explore the mysteries of his new existence.

He is amazed to learn that he has been asleep for three days of earth time. Time has no meaning here. As he becomes acclimatized, he realizes that, although this place resembles the earth, there are certain puzzling differences. There is no night, nor is there cold or rain. He is living in a perpetual summer. He cannot see the sun, but a gentle warmth permeates everything. The flowers spring up, bloom and fade away, to be replaced by others. Nothing dies or decays. There are animals, as well as his own beloved dog, but he sees none of the lower forms of life, such as the gnats and wasps that were so irritating on earth. There is a feeling of freedom and vast expanse. The fields are unbroken by fences or boundaries. On the horizon are blue hills but, no matter how far he walks, he can never reach them to see what lies beyond.

Being reunited with his family is his greatest joy, and getting to know relatives who died when he was young or before he was born. Many of his old friends are there too. Everyone in the village-like community is congenial to him. The people are of varying ages. Some who, like himself, died at an advanced age, have become younger; the years have dropped away from them. Others, like his daughter, who died young, have grown up.

There is no money here. He no longer has to go out to earn a living, since everything is provided. Shops, offices and factories have no relevance and have ceased to exist. If he wants a new suit, he has only to envisage it to find himself wearing it. No need to go to Marks and Spencers! He can relax and enjoy himself, like being on an extended holiday.

If he wishes, he can travel to other regions of the astral world. He can also visit any place on earth where he wants to go and he can certainly visit his family and friends on earth, though it may be a salutary experience, since he will find out for the first time what they really thought of him! If any of them are psychic they may be aware of his presence and, if he can find a channel of communication, he can get in touch with them and let them know that he is all right. Otherwise, if he cannot make any impression on them he may conclude that it is a waste of time to hang around any longer.

In any case, there are far more exciting things to do in his new life. He has the opportunity to pursue many of the interests and talents he didn't have time for when on earth. There are books and paintings, theatres and concert halls and places of learning where he can go to learn about the spiritual laws that govern this level of life. If he wants work to do, he can find it. He may, for instance, make it his business to assist newly arrived souls who have no one of their own to greet them.

His power to create by thought fascinates him; he is like a child with a new toy. Whatever he fancies, appears as if by the wave of a magic wand. But he discovers that these creations of his imagination have an ethereal quality. They are real and solid but at the same time he knows that they have no permanent reality. As soon as he ceases to think about them, they will cease to exist.

This is not to say that they vanish the moment he turns his back on them but they are temporary creations and will last no longer than the idea in his mind. As time goes on and he becomes more attuned to his spiritual environment his desire for materials things fades and he no longer bothers to create them. For instance, he loses his interest in food and drink, since they are not necessary here; his spiritual body draws all the nourishment it needs from the atmosphere around.

He still retains some of his familiar possessions, or the astral replica of them. Not that he really needs them, but he was attached to them on earth and is not willing to discard them yet. And he still lives in a house. True, in this place there is no need for warmth and shelter but even in the spirit world, he wouldn't feel comfortable living in the middle of a field!

His personality is gradually changing too. His fine qualities are being strengthened and his faults are diminishing. He is a better and wiser person than he was on earth, though he is still by no means perfect. But he has come a long way since the day when he left his physical body behind him. So let us leave him there for a while, and consider some of the questions that this story poses about the afterlife.

Most people's first reaction on reading the available literature about the spirit world is that it all sounds too good to be true. Can you go through this life without making any particular effort and still find yourself, after death, in a sort of paradise where everything you desire is there for the asking?

I'm sorry to disappoint you, but it's not quite as simple as that. The Summerland has to be earned. Adam Smith is reaping the fruits of the harvest he sowed on earth. His kindness, generosity and the love he showed to others have borne fruit and are now reflected in the beauty that is all around him.

Had he been a different sort of person, his fate would have been very different. The next world is not all sweetness and light. Those who have broken the spiritual laws will pay accordingly, but the crimes for which we have to atone are not always the same ones that fill jails on earth. Selfishness, cruelty, inflicting suffering upon others, deliberately seeking evil and closing the heart to good; these are the crimes against the spirit and they have to be paid for in other, darker regions of the astral world.

But even Adam was no saint. He had his faults like anyone else. Won't he have to pay for these? Yes, he will at some point have to confront the darkness in his own nature, but that will come later. For the present, he is being given time to settle in and take a rest from the trials and tribulations of earth.

Can he then, while he is at this level of existence, have literally anything he wants, just by thinking about it? Yes and no. The material of the astral is so malleable that he can mould it in accordance with his desires and he can have most of what he wants, provided that it is harmless and does not interfere with the will of others. He could for instance, have a drink or a smoke if he wanted. (I am aware that statements like this are apt to be seized upon and quoted out of context by sceptics, book reviewers and radio interviewers but that, we are told, is how it is there.) If he got tired of the perpetual sunshine he could create his own weather, as Mike Swain explains:

Whenever I need to feel the refreshing rain bearing in my face, and the wind blowing my head clear, I go out into an open field and I *think* – and then I enjoy my own private thunderstorm! It doesn't interfere with anyone else; I take good care that it doesn't; we make a point of live-and-let-live on this plane! The rain forms into little puddles as I walk; yet when I turn round and look behind me, there's no sign of it – only the usual long green grass.[3]

Should he want a change from the cottage in which he is living he can have a house designed by an architect, but it will be made of astral material, not bricks and mortar. Suppose he ardently desired a Rolls Royce. Then he could have one, but it might not be as easy to create as he thinks. Mike Swain again:

> If I want to own a brand new Jaguar, all I have to do is visualise the car in my mind, and it is created right there before my eyes, out of the thought-energy of this world! But we would think twice before doing that, because it means having to think in three dimensions! If I were to visualise the car as it looks in a magazine, that's exactly what I'd get! I need to think in terms of the width of the car, the interior of the car, all the fittings and where each rightly belongs. But Dad, the minute you think of it correctly there it is! The difficulty is to concentrate *completely* on the *whole* car, exactly as it exists.[4]

Adam might well feel it was not worth such a lot of trouble to create his Rolls Royce, especially since there are no roads and he would have nowhere to drive it!

The same applies to other technological things. Theoretically there is no reason why, say, aeroplanes, phones and televisions should not be created but, in practise no one would want them because they are not needed. Who needs a phone when it is possible to communicate over any distance by telepathy? And why have a plane when you can transport yourself instantly anywhere by thought?

There is a very sound reason why the astral world should be like this. It has been designed by a wise providence as a place where we can experience some of the things that are necessary to our development, but which we were not able to experience fully while on earth. We all leave this world with frustrated ambitions and unfulfilled longings; things we wanted to do or to try and never had the chance, or things we started and couldn't bring to fruition. We need to get these ideas out of our system, so as to speak, in order that we can be free of them before moving into the next stage.

Evil desires could not, of course, be lived out in this plane. They have to be faced up to so that they can be eradicted, but this is done on the lower levels of the astral, as we shall see later. They would have no place in the Summerland. Anyone who, for instance, harboured feelings of hatred or revenge towards another, or had no love for their fellows, would be incapable of rising to this level.

It might be objected that Adam's Summerland paradise is too tame. Suppose you preferred a more exciting environment? Then you could have it. The spirit world is as varied as this world, in fact, more so. The proviso is always that you cannot have anything you have not earned. Also, as this is a spiritual world, everyone who arrives there becomes more spiritually minded and their values change. Things that seemed important or desirable on earth no longer matter and spiritual aspirations take their place.

What is the astral body like? The answer to this, as to so many other questions about the after death world, is that it depends upon the precise level on which you are living. On the lower levels which are closer to the earth, the bodies of the inhabitants are exact replicas of their physical bodies, but as you move up towards the higher, more ethereal levels, so the body becomes more refined, although it still retains the appearance of the physical form.

Clothing is a matter of personal taste. Most people tend to wear the same sort of clothes they wore on earth because they are familiar with them – so that is what their thoughts automatically create. Others design different costumes to their own taste. Peoples of every era and culture mingle together, so it must be quite a colourful spectacle.

This being a mental world, a person's mental age is reflected in their appearance. Most people appear as they did when in the prime of their life. If they were old when they died, they gradually revert to a younger age, while a child or young person would continue to grow until they had reached maturity.

Can people really live together in such harmony? Human nature being what it is, this is one of the aspects of the Summerland most difficult to comprehend. However, by a natural law of attraction we are drawn together with those whom we have a natural affinity with, not necessarily members of our own families. The inhabitants of this realm have reached a degree of spiritual development where the petty jealousies and misunderstandings of this world have been left behind and a spirit of love prevails.

What about marriage in the spirit world? The question is often asked, when I die will I still be with my husband or wife? We are reunited with all those we love. A couple who have loved each other would still be together although, of course, the legal contract of marriage is irrelevant; it is love that holds souls together. A couple who had no real bond of affection would probably, by mutual consent, go their own ways, each being drawn to other people for whom they have a natural affinity. A person who had had more than one husband or wife would probably be with the one they had loved most, although they could all be together for in spiritual love there is no jealousy.

Which brings us on to the question of sex. Physical love becomes spiritualized, and there are no children born. Jim Pike, the son of Bishop Pike, when asked by his father whether there was sex on the other side, replied:

> Yes, there is sex, but it is not like it is here. It is not physical, of course, but actually there is less limitation. It is more obviously what sex really means. Here you can actually enter the whole person. It is like you are in fact merging, becoming one.[5]

Children grow up and are educated in schools. As they have been spared the hardships of earthly life, they become bright and beautiful souls. This following passage, from a young woman to her mother, will give comfort to anyone who has lost a child:

> Ma, I am told that children all wake up in a lovely place of their own imagining. Each child has a place of retreat locked in his own mind. It may be a picture which recalls something of his (or her) pre-natal life. In any case all children when asleep go to that sweet garden of their own minds, and they wake up on earth either refreshed by the contact, or depressed when the earth vibrations touch them and they find the contrast too great.
>
> One little boy came over with a picture of the Zoo in his mind, and so on waking he found himself back in the Zoo; but all the animals were free and friendly, and he was invited to feed them from familiar things like paper bags, and he immediately became so excited that his vision grew fast and he began to see all the other children. Some were in dream bodies, and others like himself had come over altogether.
>
> When he began to ask for Mummy and Da we told him: 'They've gone home and we'll take you home to them now if you like! On the way he fell asleep. This goes on for as long as his spirit body needs to recover. The child wakes and plays with the animals, feeds them, rides them, and sleeps alternately. One day he came upon his mother in her dream body. She was delighted

and so was he, and there was no Da. The child had adored his mother and was frightened of his father; so the joy of having his mother to himself was wonderful. When she left him to wake up to the material life, he slept. This continued for a time, most satisfying and refreshing to both.

Then one day he followed her back to her physical body, and when she woke up of course she couldn't see him. He was puzzled, but not unhappy, because they had been so much together, and one of his guides came and explained that this was Mum's world in the daytime, and he must let her go to work as usual, and await her return in the evening. Children accept this quite easily and go back to the glowing planes of childhood with immense relief. They find the earth vibrations so difficult to hold. All this makes a child's passing a very easy, happy business.[6]

Animals, too, survive and where there is great love between an owner and a pet, the pet will share the owner's afterlife. Those who die before their owners are taken care of until their owners arrive. Animals increase in intelligence and have a telepathic rapport with those around – some of them already seem to have that here! Only the higher forms of animal, those domesticated by man, are sufficiently evolved to enter the Summerland state but, having done so, they will remain there as long as their owners need and love them. After that, they return to earth to continue the course of their evolution in other bodies of the same species. The lower forms of life such as insects are not found on this level. They have souls; indeed, the whole universe is composed of living matter and nothing is truly inanimate, but their evolution keeps them closer to earth and they do not rise to this dimension.

Religion exists but is not the formalized affair it is on earth. There are churches and temples for those who want them and every religion on earth is represented. Individuals still retain difference of belief and practice but tolerance prevails. There is a natural awareness of God in everything around, a sense of being closer to his presence and enfolded in his love.

In this world, a humanitarian atheist would fare better than a bigoted Christan. There is a famous story of St Peter showing a visitor around heaven. He led him to a high, walled enclosure where, looking down, he saw a group of people happily singing and playing harps, completely oblivious of everybody else. 'Who are they?' the visitor asked. 'Oh, they're the Catholics,' Peter replied. 'They think they're the only ones here, so we have to humour them a bit!'

There is a certain amount of truth behind this story. I have said that the traditional ideas of heaven and hell are mistaken, but if someone fervently believes that when they die they are going to heaven to sit on a cloud playing a harp then they can create such a dream world for themselves – until they learn that it is a dream. The bigot who was convinced that his sect was the only one to be saved would find himself cut off in a little world of his own, shared only with like-minded believers, and here they might exist happily for hundreds of years of earth time, satisifed that their beliefs have been justified. Similarly, a person who saw himself as a wicked sinner destined for hell-fire could dream that he was among the flames, but very few people have such a low opinion of themselves; hell is always a place where one's enemies go.

What is it like to revisit the earth from the spirit side of life? Frequently very frustrating, according to what we have been told. A character called Higgins describes how he is taken by the guide who is looking after him to see his family:

The next thing I knew I was standing in our kitchen, and I was watching my wife. She was standing over the sink peeling some potatoes. I thought I wonder if she knows I'm here, and I called her name. She didn't say nothing. She didn't hear me. My friend says: 'She won't hear you, you know.'

'Well I don't know. What could I do?'

'Nothing you could do,' he says. 'But she may sense your presence. You never know. Let's just wait a little while.'

Then he says to me: 'Concentrate your thoughts on her. Just think hard. Think as hard as you can. Think her name.'

I did. And all of a sudden she stood up and looked. She dropped the knife and potato she was peeling, and she looked round. Proper bewildered she looked, almost scared. I was rather sorry in a way that I'd scared her. I realized it must have been me trying to get at her. She just flew out of that kitchen. She opened the door, and then sort of shut it again, and then she sat down, put her head on the table and started to cry. I felt awful about this. I thought, 'Oh dear, this is terrible.'

'Don't worry,' he said. 'She senses. She knows in herself, she doesn't understand yet, but she knows in herself that you're near her.'

'Well, if I'm going to make her miserable like this, there's not much point, is there?'

'Don't let that worry you,' he says, 'This often happens. They don't know with any certainty. They've never been told about the possibility of communication and all that sort of thing. But she'll come ... she senses ... she feels, and deep down in herself, deep down inside, she knows.'

'Isn't there nothing I can do?'

'Nothing,' he says. 'This is not the time.'[7]

So often the dead are cut off from the living by a wall of unbelief, but, if they do succeed in getting through, their joy is overwhelming. A young woman called Sally explains to her mother how she keeps in touch with her:

How much can I see of your life? Only when you call me into your thoughts. If you are occupied with people and things then I am also, and we are completely unconscious of one another. But the moment you think of me or something recalls me to your mind, then I see vividly all that is happening round you. You often call me, so I am constantly getting flashes of your life and interests and piecing them together ... But for many many people this is not the case at all. Either their families cease to think of them or they send such queer shut-in thoughts, full of grief and limitations. This causes great discomfort here, and we are in an agony when some people hear the thoughts of their earth links ... One of the main reasons for death and separation is that we should learn to throw our thoughts and personalities so strongly towards each other that this seemingly violent separation no longer exists.[8]

I have referred to the judgement which, at some time, each soul has to face. This judgement is not the same as the life review mentioned in near death experiences, nor is it the day of judgement, with a wrathful God sitting on a cloud meting out rewards and punishments. It is an assessment of ourselves, which we only undertake when we have been in the spirit world for some time and are in a better position, because of what we have learned, to see ourselves in a true light. We all have our dark side, thoughts and actions we are ashamed of, emotions we have repressed and we have to face these, to confront our own shadow.

This can be a painful realization, all the more so because, on the astral plane, emotions are intensified. Frances Banks, who was a nun and would, you might suppose, have had very little to reproach herself with, found it harrowing:

> During this experience the whole cycle of your life-term unfolds before you in a kaleidoscopic series of pictures. During this crisis one seems to be entirely *alone*. Yours is the judgement. You stand at the bar of your own judgement. You make your own decisions. You take your own blame. You are the accused, the judge and jury.[9]

But later, she finds that she is not in fact alone:

> Someone is beside you. Whether it is your own High Spirit or a Greater Helper I have yet to discover. Only now, as you ponder, work out, go over, tabulate and judge what you did AND WHY AND WHAT WERE THE RESULTS (good or bad) you are gloriously 'aware' of this great Being beside you, giving strength, peace, tranquillity and helping with constructive criticism. This is a wonderful experience, though harrowing at times. But very cleansing and bringing new hope.[10]

Part of the judgement process is sorting out the emotional hang-ups left over from the earthly life. T.E. Lawrence is aided in this process by a spirit helper called Mitchell, who tells him some home truths:

> He said, Your big difficulty is a scorn of slowness and impatience of mediocrity and, if you will forgive me, a really horrible feeling of superiority to most of the pleasant and ordinary people you are meeting here. They cannot avoid recognizing your reaction to them and so they keep away from you. Now how are we to get that right? I think you really feel that you ought to be able to find and meet the great people of the past whom you would perhaps regard as your equals, but my dear fellow, you are not yet fit to come near them. Look at yourself!
>
> I looked. Either I saw myself through his eyes or in some kind of immaterial mirror, but this is what I saw: shafts of keen blue light struggling to issue from a core of dark and muddled colour – a tumult of angry, murky shadow at the centre and as a response to his merciless criticism angry dartings of red flying off from it. It was not a pretty sight.

'You see,' he said gently, 'we have to clear all that before you are ready to go on.'

The shock broke me down. All my pride and unconfessed arrogance were shattered. I saw myself as less worthy than the least of these to whom I had been condescending and they must have seen it and known it as clearly as I was doing. At this crisis I fought one of my hardest battles. I subdued the angry response and begged Mitchell to go on helping me and to deal mercilessly with the faults he saw in me. A great flood of affection, warm and healing came from him to me as he replied.[11]

Lawrence finds himself, immediately after his death, in a motor-cycle accident, wandering around in a very strange world:

Before long I saw the roofs and chimneys of a small town ahead. The scene as I approached it was so like any town I might have visited on earth that the ever-present thought that this was not earth but the country of the dead began to leave me. So ordinary, so drearily earth-like were the outskirts of the hamlet; rows of small, mean houses, shops, even the usual depressing chapel I passed and so went on towards the centre which might have belonged to any English market town.

I decided to accost someone and ask for information but the passing faces had in them no signs of friendliness so I wandered on oppressed by my loneliness. True, I could now hear clearly, I could speak and sight was becoming clearer. But whether the fault of my vision or a characteristic of the locality, the same dingy murk prevailed and the place and the people were all of a piece; hard-featured women with shrill, harsh voices and men whose faces were marked by brutality and meanness came from the houses and mingled uneasily in the streets.[12]

This dreary region, which might be described as the Winterland in contrast to the Summerland, is the dwelling place of those who were not evil, but who lacked any concept of a spiritual dimension of life. When they die, they too create their own environment which reflects their inner mental state. If it seems exactly like this world, this is because they are incapable of picturing anything higher. The more materialistic a person is, the more like earth their environment appears. Souls in this lower region of the astral do not even realize they are dead, but continue to go through the motions of living just as they did on earth, eating, sleeping and going out to work. But it is a shadowy state, like a confused dream, and lacks the substance of Adam's higher plane.

It might be thought that a great many people end up here, since there are a great many people in the world who have no belief in anything spiritual, but this is not the case. We are essentially spirits; our physical body is just an outer covering, and when we die we revert to our true nature. Many people pass through this shadowland briefly, but only the hardened materialist would remain there for long.

Evil characters suffer in a hell of their own making. This region – the lowest level of the astral – is a place of darkness and cold:

> Here in these dark lands all is bleak and desolate. The very low degree of light itself casts a blight upon the whole region. Occasionally we were able to catch a glimpse of the faces of some unfortunates as we passed along. Some were unmistakably evil, showing the life of vice they had led upon the earth; some revealed the miser, the avaricious, the 'brute beast'. There were people here from almost every walk of earthly life from the present earthly time to far back in the centuries. Many of these wretches were unapproachable, and they would remain so – perhaps for numberless more centuries – until, of their own wish and endeavour, they moved however feebly in the direction of the light of spiritual progression.[13]

This hell is not a judgement from God but a self-inflicted, self-created punishment, reflecting, as on other regions, the inner mental state:

> The cruel man who had changed his natural craving for affection into a longing to give pain to others necessarily finds himself in a world where he cannot satisfy this craving. He has pandered to it during his earth life, so it has become an integral part of his soul. In the new life he has not the power to inflict pain on anything living. This means for him, with his greatly increased mental powers, a very terrible distress. He goes about seeking whom he may devour and finding naught. The misery of such an unsatisfied state is largely of a mental character. What use to him is a world of light and beauty while still this foul earth longing is unsatisfied.[14]

Souls remain in this state until they begin to feel remorse for what they have done, and then helpers are on hand to guide them towards the light. But their progress is long and painful, since they can only purge themselves by identifying with the sufferings they have caused others.

Fortunately, very few individuals are genuinely evil though some may be misguided and warped in character. For the majority of people, the next world is a happier place than this. But you may ask, if it is so easy and pleasant, doesn't it get boring in the end?

Eventually it does. The Summerland is not meant to be a permanent state. It is a place where we can rest after the earth life and get our breath back, so to speak, before passing on to a higher level of existence. Most of the communications received through mediums come from souls on this level and they do tend to give the impression that the whole of the afterlife is like this, but in fact this is just the first stage – many and glorious adventures lie ahead.

So let us return to our mythical Adam Smith. He has been in the spirit world for a number of years now. There is no compulsion to leave it – some souls remain on the astral for hundreds of years – but, content though he is, he feels an inner restlessness. The environment, which seemed such a paradise at first, is beginning to pall. He has explored its limits and exhausted its possibilities. Something within him is urging him to move on.

Those of his loved ones who are willing to accompany him go with him. The rest will remain behind, though he can return to visit them if he wishes. But for him, the dream of Summerland is over. He is ready to discover what lies beyond the blue mountains.

10 Higher Realms

Vast horizons open up before our fictitious Adam Smith as he stands on the threshold of another new world. He is now leaving the astral plane and entering the mental. From here on, his spiritual progress really begins.

As we have already noted, there is no abrupt change between one level of the spirit world and another. So, as he looks out over the scene set before him, he sees the same scenery with which he is familiar. Later, this will change but for now the trees, flowers and birds are still there to enjoy. There are houses, temples and places of learning. But he notices a subtle change in the atmosphere, a heightened sense of reality. Everything is more beautiful and is lit with a soft inner light. The forms he sees around him are no longer in human shape. They too glow with an inner radiance and this radiance forms an aura round them, clothing them like robes of many colours. There is no speech. They communicate mind to mind and soul to soul. All of them seem to be occupied, though what the nature of their work is he cannot yet understand.

As he watches, a drowsiness comes over him. He closes his eyes. He is not asleep, but drifting. His thoughts become confused. Scenes of his life in the Summerland float before him in rapid review. He feels himself being borne upwards. He is becoming lighter, freer. The light pours through him; his soul soars.

On waking, he finds himself, like those around him, clothed in a body of light. He has changed in other ways also. His consciousness has expanded. His life on earth now appears trivial, its concerns unimportant. Even the Summerland seems a dream. He is like a butterfly that has finally shed its chrysalis skin and taken wing as a free spirit.

From this higher vantage point he has a clearer view of the

laws that govern the universe. Not that he knows everything, but, taught by beings from even higher planes, he discovers answers to questions which previously he could only speculate about. The whole of his existence takes on a new perspective. He looks at it not in terms of time but of eternity. All the years of his life on earth were just a small step on the pathway of progress, a preparation for what was to come. The Summerland was a halfway stage, reflecting the beauty of the heaven world and the emotional legacy of earth. Here at last he has arrived in the pure world of spirit.

And something deep inside him recognizes this world. This was where he existed before he came to earth. It is his home, the place where he belongs, the end of all his wanderings.

His wife is still with him because there was a close spiritual affinity between them. Husbands and wives do not always stay together but, like him, she has changed from the person she was and in changing they have grown closer together, united in a spiritual union. Apart from her, his companions are no longer of his earthly family. He has been met and greeted by other souls he never knew in the physical life yet they do not feel like strangers; it is as though he has always known them. These souls, he learns, are members of his group or spiritual family. They have been drawn together by ties that go far back in time.

His links with earth are not completely broken. There is no one still living who remembers him but there are a few people, members of his group, to whom he feels he is drawn by a bond of affinity and he takes an interest in them.

He cannot do anything for them in a material sense, but he is able to help and guide them by the inspiration he channels into their minds at times when they are receptive. They may never be aware of his presence, yet his love is a strengthening and protecting influence in their lives.

This is just part of the work he does, for no one is idle on this plane and there is a great concern for the well-being of those on earth. He is taught how to use the creative mental powers he acquired on the astral plane in a higher, more selfless way. He works together with other souls and they use the power of their collective thoughts to aid the evolution of mankind, teaching and healing and sending light into all the corners of the world where there is darkness.

And there we must leave Adam Smith and his story. He is not

at the final end of his journey. There are still more mountains to climb, further planes of spirit to explore, but these regions are so far beyond anything we can comprehend that it is futile to speculate about what they may be like. In truth, he has changed so much that he is no longer the same Adam Smith who left earth so many years ago. One day he, or another facet of his being, may return to earth for another life. But before we move onto the controversial topic of reincarnation let us review what we know about the plane which he has now entered.

The mental plane is nearer God. It is not the ultimate heaven, the state of union with God, but it is heaven-like state. Chan describes it:

> Heaven is not being surrounded by people we love, although that is part of it. Heaven, real Heaven, is this indescribable untiy with a divine whole that is joy and upliftment beyond description.[1]

To enter it, the soul has to pass through a process which is known as the 'second death'. The second death involves no pain or suffering, only a short period of rest. It has been likened to the chrysalis stage in the development of a butterfly. It is a transformtion in which the soul passes from a state of consciousness that is still related to this world, to a state where all personal attachments to the earth can finally be left behind. Helen Greaves says:

> I have changed yet I have not changed. My mind is still the same, eager and thirsting for knowledge as when I was in the dimension of earth life, only now the frontiers of revelation are open and welcoming. Avenues of research lead into domains of spirit which, even in my most aspiring dreams, had never manifested themselves ... the essential remain. The unessentials are being stripped away so that the joy of the spirit remains, and an abiding peace.[2]

As in physical death the physical body is discarded, so when the second death comes the astral body, which is a replica of the physical, is shed. The soul is then clothed in a body of even finer substance which has been called the body of light. This may take human form or it may appear as pure light. Its shape and colour reflect the qualities of the soul within. But the nature of the change goes deeper than this, for with the astral body is shed the last vestige of the earthly personality.

Conan Doyle who, during his lifetime was a great protagonist of the belief in life after death, describes his second death in these words:

> The old Doyle seems to be passing, but I will prove to you all that while I die yet I live again! *But there are no trimmings left on a man when he has passed the Second Death.* Only his purified spirit remains after that supreme experience ... Oh, that second awakening! Then was I conscious of only one thing; of only one thing! – and that was the wonder, the infinitude, the allness of God's love for me and for all men.
>
> In that supreme moment I knew that there could be no such thing as separate existence apart from God. For at that moment the personality which separates man from God had died, while the individuality had been reborn. For then I saw before me a great pulsating throng of spiritual life and being, into which had passed all the souls of men who had lived in innocence and forgetfulness of self. As units of this might host of souls, those who have passed through an earth life – *which is really an earth-death* – quicken and live, giving forth from themselves with gladness and with joy all that will benefit God's mighty Plan for men.[3]

The idea that, at some point after death, the personality ceases to exist may be a disturbing one. It seems to contradict the idea that we never die, and that we will be reunited after death with those we loved. If they are no longer the same as they were here, how will we recognize them? In fact, this is not something we need to fear. It takes all but the most advanced souls many years to reach this stage. Most people spend many years on the astral, slowly learning and progressing but not changing very much, and it is there that we will be reunited with them. When there is a bond of love between two people – and, as always in spiritual law, love is the governing factor – the one in spirit will wait for the one on earth to join them, so that they can go forward together.

A group may consist of just a few souls or many and each individual within it will follow his or her own course of development but they are always bound together by spiritual ties. Sometimes on earth we meet members of our group. They may be relatives, friends or lovers or even strangers we encounter casually and feel as if we have known all our lives. Different group members will be pursuing their lives in the astral or in higher dimensions and may serve as spiritual guardians to the others. A medium's guides may be related to her in this way. Eventually, at some stage beyond death, all the members will meet and be reunited, and from this point on they will function as one. For the whole of this plane tends towards untiy, with God and with all other beings.

Direct spirit communications from the mental level are rare. The difference in the state of consciousness between this state and the earth is so great as to create an almost unbridgeable gulf. Those who try to communicate find it hard to establish their identity. Their memories of their lives on earth have faded in the way that, as we grow up, we forget many of the events of childhood. If they try to describe the conditions in which they are living, they cannot find the words in the language to express themselves.

The highest of the spirit teachers who speak through mediums come from the planes beyond the astral, but they can only utilize mediums who are able to raise their consciousness sufficiently to attune to them. In order to communicate, these teachers may assume once more the personalities they had on earth, as an actor might put on again a costume he had once worn, even though they have evolved beyond this stage of being. This is the explanation for the Red Indians, Chinamen and other exotic guides so beloved of Spiritualist mediums. The teachers are presenting themselves in a form in which they will be recognized and accepted.

Sometimes they work in conjunction with other souls who are still on the astral plane, who act as messengers or mediators, enabling them to bridge the gulf. Thus all levels of creation, from the highest to the lowest, are linked together, like Jacob's ladder, with links of golden light.

If the spirit world is such a beautiful place, why should anyone want to leave it to come back to earth? The question is often asked and of course, not everyone who believes in life after death believes that we do come back. Reincarnation has never figured much in the teachings of Spiritualism, which is mainly concerned with the stage of life just after this, although it is a major tenet of Spiritism, the branch of Spiritualism which was founded in the last century by Allan Kardec and which has many followers in Brazil and other countries.

However, in recent years there has been a gradual change in attitude among Spiritualists and mediums in this country and America, and many more people are coming round to this way of thinking. The Eastern religions have been teaching reincarnation for thousands of years. It was taught by many of the early church fathers and was a widely held belief in the Christian church, until it was outlawed by the Council of Nicea in AD 325. The general consensus among the spirit teachers is that reincarnation is a fact, though one or two of them deny this – but there are differences of opinion and belief in the next world as well as this.

Certainly, the evidence for it is very strong. One of the most famous researchers in this field, Dr Ian Stevenson, has published accounts of a number of cases of apparent past life recall in his book *Twenty Cases Suggestive of Reincarnation*. There is, for example, the case of a boy called Ravi Shankar.

Ravi Shankar was born in 1951 in Kannauj, near Kanpur, India, the son of Sri Babu Ram Gupta. From his early years he told his parents that he had memories of another life, when he had been the son of Jageshwar Orasad, a barber of the Chhipatti district of Kannauj. He claimed that, in that life, he had been murdered at the age of six by two neighbours so that one of the murderers – a relative of his father – might inherit the father's property. Ravi gave details of where and how he had been killed and his mother testified that he had a mark on his neck closely resembling the scar of a long knife. The man who Ravi said had been his father in that previous life visited the boy, and confirmed that the details he gave were correct.

More evidence for reincarnation was collected by the hypnotherapist Arnall Bloxham, who regressed 400 subjects, under hypnosis, back to their past lives. These cases were investigated by a television producer, Jeffery Iverson, and subsequently published in the book *More Lives Than One*. One subject recalled a life as a Jewish woman, Rebecca, in York in the twelfth century. She described a massacre in which she and her family were killed. Iverson compared her account with what is known historically of the events and the details were found to be impressively accurate. One thing could not be traced.

'Rebecca' claimed that she and her family had hidden from their persecutors in the crypt of a church. The details she gave suggested that this could only have been St Mary's Church, Castlegate, close to the castle. The problem was that, as far as anyone knew, neither this nor any of the churches that would have been standing at the time had a crypt. Yet six months later, workmen restoring St Mary's dug under the chancel – and found the remains of one.

Accounts such as this cannot be dismissed as fantasizing on the part of the subjects, nor can they be explained by cryptomnesia, the theory (nothing to do with crypts!) that, under hypnosis, the subject is recalling memories from the present lifetime that have been hidden in the subconscious. The intensity with which the subjects relive their past life experiences is what convinces many investigators of their validity. Indeed, anyone who has spontaneously recalled a past life, either under hypnosis or in a state of meditation, will know how vivid it can be and what a deep impact it makes emotionally.

The subject of reincarnation is a complex one. To explore all its ramifications would take us outside the scope of the present book, but it is interesting to consider the teachings that have been received on the subject through various mediums and how this relates to the whole question of what happens in the world beyond death.

We speak of coming back to earth many times, as if we travel round and round in endless circles from this world to the next and back again; the wheel of rebirth, that never stops turning. People are apt to say, 'I was a priestess in a former life' or 'I was a Roman general.' No one seems to admit that they were a slave or a road sweeper! In fact, leaving aside the fantasies of those who claim to have been Cleopatra or the Queen of Sheba, this commonly held view of reincarnation is over-simplified.

I like to use the analogy of a wheel, but in a different way. The hub of the wheel is the higher self of which I spoke earlier, the true centre of our being. This higher self never fully incarnates; it remains in the higher spiritual realms to which it belongs. But from time to time it sends down to earth a facet of itself, like a spoke of the wheel. Each of these spokes or facets is a separate personality. The personality grows up, develops and eventually passes out of the physical body in death. After death it continues to live on in the astral world, and it may still be unaware that it is part of a greater whole, until it rises to a higher level of consciousness at which it becomes one with the greater being.

The higher self then puts forth another facet, another spoke of the wheel, to live on earth and gain fresh experiences. All these experiences it absorbs into itself, thus gaining wisdom and knowledge.

When a child is born it already has a definite personality, as any parent will know who has had to battle with a highly vocal and determined infant. Heredity obviously plays a major part in this but it cannot entirely account for it. Even identical twins may have very different personalities. Of course, the character will be shaped by the child's upbringing and environment but these only mould what was there to start with.

In the case of some children, this is very clear. You can look into their eyes and feel instinctively that they are an 'old soul,' one that has had many lives and is possessed of a wisdom beyond its years. Children themselves sometimes have a sense of being alien, as if they do not belong in this world or want to be here. I well remember, when I was very young, feeling that I was already an adult, imprisoned in a small body, and bitterly resenting being treated as a child.

We think of death as something to be feared, but in fact the evidence suggests that being born is a worse trauma than dying. As people who have had near death experiences often say that they did not want to leave the place they were in to return to the body, so those who have been regressed to the period between lives frequently speak of their reluctance to be born.

The American psychologist Helen Wambach conducted a study in which she regressed a number of the students to the time before they were born and asked them a series of questions including, 'How do you feel about the prospect of living this coming lifetime?' Many of her subjects experienced a sense of sorrow. One woman commented, 'I felt such compassion for that baby who was me. I felt such sadness to leave the place where I was to come back into physical life. It seemed so hard to be confined in a little body, and to lose the lightness and the love I had known in the between-life state.'[4]

So why do we choose to come? Helen Wambach's students spoke of the need to gain more experience or to learn some necessary lesson, and this is the reason given by many teachers from spirit. It seems that we have to return to earth many times

because we cannot undergo all the experiences we need in one
lifetime. We need to know riches and poverty, hardship and ease
and to live in different ages and cultures. We also need to see
life both from the masculine and the feminine point of view, so
we come back sometimes as a man and sometimes as a woman;
the spirit within has no sex.

The soul chooses when it will come, but the choice is made in
consultation with others, including members of the soul group.
It is interesting that many of Helen Wambach's subjects spoke
of being guided in their decision by counsellors. One said:

> Yes, I chose to be born, and there seemed to be four or so
> entities around me advising me about the coming lifetime. My
> feelings about living in the coming lifetime were that I wanted to.
> I felt that this is an important lifetime and my counsellors were
> insistent that I come in this time period.[5]

We also select our parents, who are frequently souls we have
known before. The people who are important in our lives;
families, husbands, wives and close friends, are often those we
have known in the past, but it is not necessarily love that draws
us back to them. We may be brought together again because
there is something we have to work out together, some old
enmity, hatred or resentment. This is one reason why human
relationships are so difficult!

The course of our life is not predestined but we do come back
with some sort of blueprint, a general idea of what is in store for
us and what we need to accomplish, and this knowledge is
retained at a subconscious level. Indeed, the memory of all our
past lives is stored deep in the subconscious. Perhaps it's just as
well we don't consciously remember. It's bad enough having to
live with all the things we've done wrong in this life, without
being burdened with the memory of our misdeeds in the murky
past! Sometimes recollections do come back spontaneously,
perhaps when we visit a place and know we have been there
before, or meet a stranger and feel as if we are meeting an old
friend – or enemy. And whether or not we are aware of it, our
past lives do affect us. They have made us what we are today.
Some psychological and health problems which have no obvious
cause in the present may have their roots in previous
incarnations. This is demonstrated by regression therapy, a

process by which patients are helped to recall past lives under hypnosis.

There seems to be no rule as to how long a soul spends in the spirit realm between lives. Some may come back soon after death, particularly if their earthly life was cut short. Others who had a long or difficult life may spend a long while recuperating. Some souls may choose not to reincarnate at all, as the spirit teacher Ramadan explains:

> There are certain cleansings undertaken by some spirits who feel responsible for the errors of a past experience so some return in a body while others stand by and help. Spirits also enter the atmosphere of earth to work through a medium or to use one as a channel through whom blessing may be released, as with those dedicated to nursing, healing or surgery, or of work in which they try to lead a body of people unto greater truth. In doing these things each will find he has to contend with earth's ignorance, dissensions if he is a priest or teacher, selfishness and hatred if a leader of a nation. But each, as they fulfil their work, will have around them a group of spirits who are also engaged in trying to cleanse the earth of its weight of woe.[6]

Reincarnation makes sense of the apparent injustices of life. It explains why some people sail through life with no worries while others, apparently more deserving, suffer all kinds of hardships and problems. The law of Karma teaches that we reap what we have sown. If we do wrong in one life, then we must pay for it in another. There is no escaping the consequences of our actions. Karma is rather like the Inland Revenue. You may think you've got away with it, but it always catches up with you in the end.

There is nothing arbitrary about Karma. It is the natural law of cause and effect. If we have caused suffering to another, we will suffer ourselves at some time in the future. Our own misdeeds rebound on us like a boomerang and the trials we endure in life – disease, misfortune and heartache – are usually things we have brought upon ourselves. But even suffering has its value:

> The events in your lives, sometimes of bitterness and despair, of pain and misery, all play their part in preparing the soul gradually for the path that is being trodden.
> The darkness and the light, the shadow and the sunshine, are

all but reflections of one whole. Without shadow there could be no light and without light there could be no shadow. The difficulties of life are steps which enable the soul to rise. Difficulties, obstacles, handicaps – these are the trials of the soul. And when it conquers them all, it rises stronger, more purified, deepened in intensity and more highly evolved.

Do you think that the latent powers of the soul, infinite in their possibilities of expression, could realise themselves without difficulty and pain, without shadow, without sorrow, and without suffering and misery? Of course not.

The joy and the laughter can only be enjoyed to the full when once you have drained the cup of sorrow to the dregs, for as low as you can fall in the scale of life so correspondingly you can rise. The more you have tasted and experienced that which seems the shadow of earthly life, the more you will appreciate, because of it, the greater joys of the sunshine.

Your experiences are all part of your evolution. One day, freed from the trammels of flesh, with eyes not clouded by matter, you will look back in retrospect and view the life you have lived on earth. And out of the jigsaw of all the events, you will see how every piece fits into its allotted place, how ever experience was a lesson to quicken the soul and to enable it to have greater understanding of its possibilities.[7]

There comes a time, probably after countless incarnations, when the soul has no need to return to earth again. It has learned all the lessons the earth has to teach and, while it is still not a perfect being, it has earned its release from this heavy and frequently painful level of existence.

After that, it may still return, of its own free will, in order to be of service to mankind, like the compassionate Buddha who refused to enter Nirvana until the last blade of grass had been redeemed. Or it may leave the earth behind for ever, progressing to even higher planes of spirit.

Will we ever meet Jesus, many Christians want to know? The spirit teachers hold Jesus in great respect, seeing him as perhaps the greatest teacher and healer ever to have walked the earth and they claim that his mission did not end with his physical death, but that he continues to guide mankind from the spirit world.

We are told that Jesus and other great masters inhabit regions beyond the mental plane. Conan Doyle describes these realms:

It is in the *celestial* world that the world of creation really begins. That is the glory and magnificence of the celestial world, and of its creative art which is the real *becoming* of all creation. In this heaven world the soul of man absorbs a potency from the divine quality of Christ; having itself become almost angelic, it dwells among angelic beings sharing their lustre. Would that we could endow you with some flash of intuition or insight which would reveal a glimpse of the harmony, the perfection and the glory of this heaven life! For it is here that the soul of man becomes conscious at last of its true nature, here that the ego knows itself a very part of God.[8]

These angelic beings have an immense compassion for mankind and are constantly reaching down into this world. Occasionally one of them may make the great sacrifice of incarnating on earth, and these are the true saints of the world. They may be religious leaders or they may lead obscure lives but in whatever walk of life they are found, their light radiates from them and touches all those around.

It is hard to think that we may one day reach this state of development ourselves though we are told by the spirit world that this is our ultimate destiny. But we will then still be ourselves? Or will we lose our individuality and merge into God, like a drop of water slipping into the ocean? The teachers assert that we never lose our own identity. White Owl, the guide of Stephen O'Brien, says:

I would have been on this side of life for many, many years, as you would gauge time, and I have heard of no one who has 'lost' or 'diffused' their individuality back into the Godhead from whence it came.

Once individuality has been characterized, it seems for ever established.

Often I am privileged to take counsel with many great teachers – the Ancient Shining Ones – who are aware of all our thoughts and the work we are undertaking through mediums on earth. They come to instruct and guide us, and they teach that greater awareness of individuality will be afforded to the soul as it progresses towards the Light. They do not speak of annihilation, back to a primordial source.

But that is not to say we will always have an outward tangible vehicle of expression, for eventually we will have no need of this.

I have communed with some greatly advanced souls who have

remained perfectly individual in their essence, but who have no
outward form of any kind. They are points of consciousness,
pure thought and feeling: time and space is open to them – they
are very evolved indeed.

But I am speaking now of souls who have existed here for
aeons, and not newcomers who have been here a mere few
thousand years.

A mere few thousand years! It is hard enough sometimes for us
to think ten or twenty years ahead; the mind boggles at the
contemplation of aeons of time. But of course, time has no
meaning in infinity.

So what is the purpose of our existence? White Eagle
summarizes it:

> In the beginning man was born, or *breathed forth* from the Holy of
> Holies, or from the 'womb' of Love, Wisdom and Power. He was
> then entirely pure and innocent of soul. Now he is destined to
> learn to conquer weakness, to control matter, to overcome
> temptation. That is why he is here.
>
> In this connection the story or legend of Atlas who carried the
> world on his shoulders is still significant; for it pictures the soul
> of man taking upon itself all the weight of worldliness. This
> burden is laid upon every soul, a burden which gradually
> increases until at the lowest arc of its evolution the soul is
> completely weighed down. At this stage it seems to be quite
> unaware of spheres of beauty and truth from which it came forth
> and to which it will eventually return.[9]

One day we will return to our origins. But it makes no sense to
ask what lies at the end of the journey, for in truth there is no
end. Spiritualism teaches that there is eternal progress open to
every human soul. Only one thing we can be sure of; that the
higher we travel in the realms of spirit, the more love,
compassion and beauty we shall find.

> Life is eternal and love is immortal and death is only an horizon,
> and an horizon is nothing save the limit of our sight.

11 Mediumship in the New Age

It is now nearly 150 years since the foundation of the modern Spiritualist movement in America. What has it achieved in that time and how might it develop in the future?

The story of how Spiritualism began is well-known. It started in Hydesville, New York State, in 1848 when two sisters by the name of Fox made contact with the ghost haunting their family's farmhouse. Using a code of raps, they established that he was a pedlar who had been murdered in the house a few years before. News of the incident spread and led to a craze for table-rapping that rapidly engulfed America and, like most things American, soon found its way to Britain. Soon everyone was trying to get in touch with the spirits. It was a bizarre way to launch a new religion and the banal messages, rapped out in dark rooms, hardly seemed to promise a new spiritual revelation.

Yet it was an important breakthrough. Ghosts and apparitions had been around since the beginning of time and there had always been mediums, even if they were called by other names but now, for the first time, ordinary men and women could reach out beyond the grave and make contact not with vague, frightening spectres but with individuals they knew and recognized. No longer did they have to rely on priests to tell them when the afterlife was life. As methods of communication improved, they could receive the first-hand accounts of the dead themselves. For those who accepted the new teaching, faith was replaced by knowledge and hope by certainty.

The significance of this is overlooked today. We are accustomed to the idea of seeking our own truth rather than accepting the received wisdom of the past. The basic idea of communication with the beyond – though still rejected by many – is familiar to everyone. But in the 1840s, it was a revolutionary concept. A door had been opened in man's psyche that would never be closed again.

It is easy to ridicule the Spiritualism of the Victorian age, or of our own age, for that matter. It does have its absurd aspect; phantom forms floating about in ectoplasm robes, little old ladies sitting in dark rooms trying to call up the dead. And some mediums really are like Madame Arcati. No one can deny either that the history of mediumship is marred by fraud. Human nature being what it is, it was inevitable that unscrupulous imposters should set themselves up to take advantage of the gullible.

But let us look on the positive side also. Over the years, millions of people have been comforted and their grief eased by the contact established with those they thought they had lost. There have been many fine and dedicated mediums who have fought for their cause, often against severe persecution. Thanks to their efforts, the knowledge of life after death is now freely available for anyone who chooses to seek it.

Spiritualism has failed to convince the scientists, despite the impressive body of evidence that has been built up over the last century and a half, much of which now lies gathering dust in the archives of the Society for Psychical Research. This is, no doubt, only to be expected. Scientists as a whole adhere to the materialism that took root towards the end of the Victorian age; the fallacy that nothing exists that cannot be seen, analysed or captured in a test-tube.

However, there are hopeful signs that this is changing. A new generation of physicists is emerging who are taking a holistic view of the universe, seeing it as a living organism in which all the parts are closely related, an attitude that brings them strangely into line with ancient mystical teachings.

There are hints – no more than tantalizing clues at present – that this new view of science may explain much that, in the past, was regarded as supernatural and may in fact hold the key to the invisible world. The theory of quantum mechanics has led to a questioning of our basic assumptions about the nature of reality. It has been discovered that the sub-atomic particles of which the universe is made up are not solid, but are fluid substances that can take on the nature of waves or particles, the form they adopt being dependent upon the observer. These particles are able to affect each other over space, even when they are not in contact, a phenomenon that Einstein referred to appropriately as 'spooky action at a distance.' Somewhere here may lie the rationale behind telepathy and clairvoyance.

Moreover, it now appears that nine-tenths of the mass of which the universe is composed is beyond the range of our physical senses. This may include the non-physical planes of life where, we are told, matter can be moulded by the power of mind and we create our own reality by our thoughts – a concept which is now becoming less like a mystical abstraction and more like a tenable scientific theory.

I believe that, in time, the phenomena of the séance room, the materialization and dematerialization of matter, the existence of life beyond death and many other mysteries for which there is at present no generally accepted explanation will be understood in a scientific way that makes them plausible to the age we live in. When this happens, the age-old conflict between science and belief will disappear. Any scientists who still cling to the old, materialistic view will find themselves out of step with modern thinking, and those who believe in the supernatural but are afraid to risk their reputations by saying so will be able to come out into the open. Scientists and believers will then be able to work together to deepen our knowledge of the universe and solve the mysteries that have baffled mankind for centuries.

The fact that parapsychology is now becoming almost a respectable branch of science is a step in the right direction, though parapsychology tends to see everything in terms of the earthly mind and, since it discounts the possibility of the soul or discarnate existence, it does not concern itself with spirit communication. Some organizations however, are continuing to do research in this field.

One of these is ASSAP, The Association for the Scientific Study of Anomalous Phenomena. Founded in 1981, its purpose is to 'investigate and research areas of human experience and observed phenomena for which no generally accepted explanation yet exists' and it looks into everything from apparitions to UFOs. Members are expected to adopt a scientific attitude, but not a negative one. ASSAP runs seminars and training courses and has over 300 members and a number of local groups, who are encouraged to report on their encounters with the unexplained.

Another research organization is the Survival Joint Research Committee Trust. This was set up in 1963 with the aim of stimulating co-operation between psychical research and the international Spiritualist movement. It consists of a small team of trustees and advisory consultants whose chairman is Dr Michael Coleman. Members are elected and are chosen for their sympathetic attitude to both the scientific and the Spiritualist point of view.

The secretary of the Trust, Dennis Bury, told me, 'We keep a very low profile. This area of research is riddled with a lot of tension. We try to bridge the gulf between belief and science.'

The Trust refrains from committing itself on the results of the research it has carried out. Psychical researchers like to hedge their bets and are always looking for alternative explanations for the evidence produced by mediums. The most popular of these, and one that has been around since the last century, is the super ESP theory. According to this, the medium is, by a process of unconscious telepathy, drawing all her information out of the mind of the sitter. This explanation can by extension be made to fit any contingency and explain away almost any evidence. If the information given is within the knowledge of any living person, even if that person is unknown to the medium and has no connection with the sitter, and even if they are on the other side of the world, then it can be claimed that the medium may have picked it up telepathically. Should it exist anywhere in written form it can be alleged that they picked it up by clairvoyance.

However, as Dennis Bury pointed out, if communication with the next world has never been conclusively proved, then neither has super ESP. And the Trust has come up with an experiment designed to rule this explanation out.

Before their deaths, various members of the Trust had specially designed padlocks made which could only be opened by someone who knew the combination. They promised to try to communicate these combinations from the other side. So far they have had no success but the task is a difficult one. Communication is not easy and it is particularly hard to convey a series of random numbers. Attempts are still going on, and the Trust may still get the proof it is looking for.

The Society for Psychical Research, whose pioneering investigations into mediumship made such an important contribution to the study of the subject in the last century and the early part of this, now concentrates most of its efforts in other fields of research. However, a test similar to the padlock test of the Survival Trust was set up a few years ago.

Dr Robert Thouless of Cambridge University, who died in 1984, left behind him two coded sequences. His intention was to communicate the keys to decipher them. The only clues he left are that the key to the first is a continuous passage of poetry or prose which may be indicated by referring to its title, and the key to the second consists of two words.

The sequences are as follows:

INXPH CJKGM JIRPR FBCVY WYWES NOECN SCVHE GYRJQ TEBJM TGXAT TWPNH CNYBC FNXPF LFXRV QWQL

and

BTYRR OOFLH KCDXK FWPCZ KTADR GFHKA HTYXO ALZUP PYPVF AYMMF SDLR UVUB.

So far, although many attempts have been made, no one has come up with the right answers but the SPR is always pleased to hear from anyone who thinks they might have cracked the code. Answers on a postcard please.

From its beginnings in America, Spiritualism has now spread all over the world. In continental Europe, although there are hardly any Spiritualist churches, there are many psychic centres and groups. One country where there is a tremendously strong interest is Iceland, and many British mediums are invited there to work. In Australia, where until fairly recently Spiritualism was illegal, there are now many churches.

Spiritualism has developed in a very different way in Brazil. Here, the movement is called Spiritism and is based on the teachings of the nineteenth century Frenchman, Allan Kardec. One of its principle tenets is reincarnation. Although Brazil is officially a Roman Catholic country, Spritism exists side by side with Roman Catholicism, which is obliged to tolerate it because of its great following – the majority of the population follow some form of Spiritist belief.

Brazil is a very poor country and the Spiritist church does a great deal of social work, running hospitals, schools and orphanages. In Britain, Brazil is best known for its psychic surgeons but it has many remarkable mediums, some of whom are world famous. A few years ago I met Franco Divaldo, a trance medium who had been all over the world lecturing. He has written many spirit-inspired books and claims that one of his comunicators is Victor Hugo. Like many Brazilian mediums, Franco takes no money for his work but devotes the proceeds to the children's mission he has founded, where he has legally adopted 192 children.

Another spirit-inspired writer, Chico Xavier, is Brazil's most prolific author. He has written in trance over 250 books, on subjects ranging from science to literature, which he claims were dictated to him by deceased Brazilian and Portuguese writers. Xavier now does little public work because of his age and ill health but a new medium, Raoul Teixeira, is now becoming well-known in Brazil and beyond.

There are many different levels within Spiritism. Communication with recently deceased loved ones is provided by mediums who work in trance or through automatic writing, rather than by giving public demonstrations of clairvoyance such as we have here. Healing and prayer also play an important role and many Spiritists are more concerned with the higher aspect, valuing mediums who are able to link with evolved spirit teachers rather than those who produce phenomena.

Janet Duncan, who lived for some years in Brazil and now runs the London based Allan Kardec Study Group, explained to me, 'Spiritism looks beyond the proof of survival to the end goal, the striving towards perfection, which is, after all, what we are all in this life to try to achieve.' The study group consists mainly of Brazilians resident in this country but anyone who is interested is welcome to attend their meetings, although, as Janet told me, 'We're a very small group. Most people find the emphasis we put on inner reform too difficult and demanding.'

In America, according to many British mediums I have spoken to who regularly work there, there is a large Spiritualist movement, but the standard of mediumship is generally much lower than in this country. America has produced a new phenomenon – channelling. Like the table-tapping mania of the last century, channelling has become a fast growing fashion, the books of Shirley MacLaine having done much to assist its growth.

Channelling is, of course, nothing new but the Americans like to think they invented it. It started to be popular some twenty or thirty years ago. One of the first channellers was Jane Roberts, whose 'Seth' books (Seth being the name of the entity she channelled) have become classics of their kind. Since then, books have poured off the presses, some thought-provoking, containing philosophical insights, some bizarre, many mediocre. One of the most influential is *A Course in Miracles*, channelled by Helen Cohn Schuman. This book, which has sold hundreds of thousands of copies and been translated into several languages, contains instructions for a series of spiritual exercises which many readers claim have transformed their lives.

It is often assumed that 'channelling' (which the Americans spell with one 'l') is the modern term for mediumship, but this is an oversimplification. Coral Polge, on a recent visit to America, was startled to be asked, 'Who do you channel?' It is not a question which she would have been asked in this country and shows the different concept that exists in the States.

Channellers are trance mediums; they 'bring through' a particular spirit entity who, in some cases, become more famous than the medium themselves. In Britain, although there are a few well-known trance mediums who serve as a vehicle for a spirit teacher, trance itself is unusual. In America, mediums tend to work within the Spiritualist movement and to concentrate on giving personal 'messages' as they do in this country, whereas channellers work outside it, and in fact dislike being associated with the organized churches.

The words 'medium' and 'channel' are defined in different ways by different people. Generally speaking, however, a 'medium' is someone who communicates with individuals recently deceased. 'Channelling' is a broader term and encompasses communication from any source outside oneself.

Channellers claim to receive their material from various sources. These include 'ascended masters' – advanced souls who no longer need to incarnate on earth (as Jesus is said to be) and beings from other planets or from non-human levels of existence. Such claims are, by their nature, impossible to verify and the value of what is communicated can only be judged by those who receive it. No doubt much 'comes through' that is true and helpful, and indeed some of the teaching received deserves to be studied and contains much wisdom and beauty. But much is merely the medium's subconscious mind, which accounts for some of the more bizarre sources. One medium channels dolphins. Obviously, discernment is needed – and not always applied. The followers of Elizabeth Clare

Prophet packed up their bags last year and moved to bomb shelters in a remote corner of Oregon in preparation for the nuclear war they had been told was imminent. At the time of writing, they're still there.

Is channelling going to be the way forward for mediums in this country? In view of its obvious dangers, I hope not. Without proper understanding or training of the gift of trance, imagination can easily run riot and the meaningless drivel spoken by a so-called channeller in a self-induced trance can be solemnly accepted as the infallible utterances of a superhuman master. And some people will believe anything if they think it comes from the other side.

Spiritualism in this country has always concentrated on establishing contact with those who have recently died, as a means of providing evidence that life continues after death and of comforting those left behind. Its aim has been to produce convincing evidence, which cannot easily be explained away. Even though it often falls short of this ideal, this is still seen as the medium's function.

However, talking to Spiritualists today and going around the churches, I am aware of a growing dissatisfaction with this limited view of mediumship. No one denies that it still has its place. There will always be new people coming along who perhaps have been recently bereaved and who are seeking their own personal proof of life beyond death, and indeed more mediums are needed who are trained to a high standard so that they can provide this. But I've heard it said time and time again, from regular church-goers, 'I don't need any more proof and I'm not really interested in clairvoyance. So where do I go from here?'

Unfortunately, it is always hard to answer that question. Some churches do offer lectures or discussion groups, as do centres such as the Spiritualist Association of Great Britain and the College of Psychic Studies. In this connection, the White Eagle Lodge should be mentioned. The Lodge, which has temples in London and Hampshire, is not a Spiritualist organization as such although it bases its teachings upon the teachings of a guide called White Eagle and the emphasis is on teaching and meditation. But, on the whole, Spiritualism suffers from a lack of teachers and mediums able to expound its philosophy.

Spritualism was a dynamic movement in the nineteenth

century and was a forerunner of the New Age of which we hear so much now, which embraces many different philosophies. But in many ways it is still anchored in the last century. The structure of the movement, with churches that offer conventional style services (except for the demonstrations of clairvoyance) is off-putting for many people who associate churches with weddings, funerals and boring sermons. Speaking personally as an organist, I love services with music, but I recognize that not everyone shares my tastes.

Some Spiritualists feel that psychic centres would better answer the needs of the public today; places where people could meet socially as well as having groups for teaching or discussion and where mediums could be available for private consultations. This is one possible way forward. Such centres need not replace churches, and in fact could use the same premises, so as to cater for the needs of all kinds of people.

Perhaps in this respect it could learn a lot from studying the way things are done in Brazil, with its centres for teaching, healing and prayer. For Spiritualism is a religion and, in my view, we should not lose sight of that fact. We do not need to have formal ceremonies and many people today feel more at ease with quiet meditation than with formal prayers and hymn-singing. But prayer, in some form, needs to play a part. Spiritualism is all about developing our own spirituality and raising our consciousness in order to bring out the highest that is within us. Without this, it is in danger of becoming mere psychism, having little contact with God and, ultimately, little contact with the spirit world either.

I find it encouraging that an increasingly large number of mediums are refusing to confine themselves to traditionally accepted methods of working and are using their gifts in broader context. Some are undertaking counselling work, which is at best a form of healing. The New Age is producing an increasing number of people who are psychic in one way or another and need help to come to terms with this facet of their personalities and the difficulties their sensitivity may be causing in their lives. Of course, many different types of counselling and therapy are now available, but mediumship has a unique contribution to make in assisting those whose particular talents, or difficulties, lie in their instinctive openness to the invisible world. Such people rarely come seeking proof of life after death. Their own experiences and intuitive awareness have convinced them of that already. They are looking beyond this, and beyond the astral level of the spirit world, to find something more profound.

Other mediums are moving into the area of regression therapy. This is an interesting development, partly because, until a few years ago, the idea of reincarnation was not generally accepted among Spiritualists (some of whom frown upon it now). One medium who has chosen to work in this way is Judy Hall of the College of Psychic Studies. She combines her insight as a medium with her knowledge of astrology, to reach back into her clients' past lives, in order to uncover the roots of traumas and assist them to a better understanding of their inner selves.

Mediumship could also prove to be of value in the treatment of mental illness. Important pioneering work in this field was carried out in the early part of this century by Dr Carl Wickland. With the assistance of his wife, who was a medium, he claimed that, in some cases, he had contacted spirits who were possessing his patients and had been able to release them, thus restoring the patient to health. Since then a few psychiatrists have acknowledged that certain cases of schizophrenia or multiple personality may have a psychic component, even if they would not necessarily accept the spirit hypothesis. It is interesting to note that these secondary personalities sometimes display power of clairvoyance or precognitive abilities which the patients do not display in their normal state.

I am not for a moment suggesting that all mental illness is due to spirit possession – obviously we should not underestimate the strange feats the human mind is capable of. What I am suggesting, however – and mediums such as Terry O'Sullivan would no doubt agree – is that, where the mind has been damaged by some childhood trauma which has caused certain parts of the personality to split off, the patient may be vulnerable to invasion by discarnate entities. This makes for a complex situation, where it is hard to tell which personalities are products of the patient's subconscious and which are disembodied entities.

This subject is examined at depth in D. Scott Rogo's book *The Infinite Boundary*, which describes the work of Dr Ralph Allison, a leading authority on multiple personality. Dr Allison is one of the few modern psychiatrists to state openly his belief in the possibility of spirit possession. Most psychiatrists dismiss the notion as a return to medieval superstition and regard mediums as themselves suffering from schizophrenia or some hallucinatory disorder. But now that conventional medicine is becoming more willing to work side by side with spiritual healing and other forms of alternative therapies, hopefully mediums and psychiatrists might work together in the future to help those who are afflicted in this way.

To end on a personal note. As a medium, I am so accustomed to the ideas of spirit communication that I take it for granted, until it comes home to me in a very intense way how much comfort it can give.

During the course of writing this book my mother died. Although she had been ill for some months I was not expecting her to pass away as soon as she did. I should perhaps have foreseen it but mediums often don't foresee things that affect them most closely.

I was not aware of her presence immediately after she had died. I was told by my spirit helpers that she was resting, which is quite usual for old people or those who have suffered from a long or debilitating illness. A couple of days after her death, I was sitting alone in the room where she used to sit, thinking about her, when I heard a miaow at the French windows. It was the black cat from next door, scrounging for food. It is actually a very well fed cat but, like most felines, can't resist cadging an extra titbit.

My mother was very fond of birds and used to feed them from that window. Fearing that the cat might catch them, she used to chase it away. But I love cats, so I opened the window and called it.

It was about to come in when it suddenly stopped short, looked past me at something in the room that I couldn't see then arched its back, hissed and ran off. Yes, I thought. Mother's around. And what's more, she hasn't changed a bit!

Since then she's become very close to me and we've been able to sort out our differences over one or two little things we didn't see eye to eye about. I don't cling to her. She has a new life to get on with. But I know she'll never be far away, and that one day we will meet again. It doesn't matter that I wasn't there at the very end to say goodbye to her. Knowing that life goes on, I know that we never need to say goodbye.

The next world and the next; life is a continuous progress, always moving further along the pathway to light, love and understanding; along a road that has no end.

Notes

Chapter 8

1 Barrett, Sir William, *Death-Bed Visions* (1926) (Aquarian Press, 1986)
2 Cummins, Geraldine, *Swan on a Black Sea* (Routledge & Kegan Paul, 1965)
3 Rosher, Grace, *The Traveller's Return* (Psychic Press, 1968)
4 Hamilton, Margaret Lillian, *Is Survival A Fact?* (Psychic Press, 1969)
5 Dawson Scott, C.A., *From Four Who Are Dead* (Arrowsmith, 1926)
6 Sandys, Cynthia & Lehmann, Rosamond, *The Awakening Letters* (Vol. 1, Neville Spearman, 1978)
7 Sherwood, Jane, *Post-Mortem Journal* (Neville Spearman, 1964)
8 Randall, Neville, *Life After Death* (Robert Hale, 1975)
9 Turoff, Stephen, *Seven Steps to Heaven* (Elmore-Chard, 1990)
10 Swain, Jasper, *On the Death of My Son* (Turnstone Press, 1974)
11 Ortzen, Tony, ed., *Silver Birch Companion* (Psychic Press, 1986)
12 Grey, Margot, *Return From Death* (Arkana, 1985)

Chapter 9

1 Swedenborg, Emanuel, *Heaven and Its Wonders and Hell* (Swedenborg Society, 1958)
2 Borgia, Anthony, *Life in the World Unseen* (Odhams Press, 1954)
3 Swain, Jasper, *op. cit.*
4 *Ibid.*
5 Pike, James, A., *The Other Side* (Abacus, 1975)
6 Sandys, Cynthia & Lehmann, Rosamond, *Letters from Our Daughters* (College of Psychic Studies)
7 Randall, Neville, *op. cit.*
8 Sandys, Cynthia & Lehmann, Rosamond, *op. cit.*
9 Greaves, Helen, *Testimony of Light* (Neville Spearman, 1969)
10 *Ibid.*
11 Sherwood, Jane, *op. cit.*
12 *Ibid.*
13 Borgia, Anthony, *op. cit.*
14 Cummins, Geraldine, *The Road to Immortality* (Psychic Press, 1967)

Chapter 10

1 Northage, Ivy, *Journeys Beyond: Trance Talks by Chan* (Psychic Press, 1988)
2 Greaves, Helen, *op. cit.*
3 Cooke, Ivan, *The Return of Sir Arthur Conan Doyle* (White Eagle Publishing Trust, 1956)
4 Wambach, Helen, *Life Before Life* (Bantam, 1979)
5 *Ibid.*
6 Roberts, Ursula, *Wisdom of Ramadahn* (Psychic Press, 1956)
7 Austen, William, ed., *Teachings of Silver Birch* (Psychic Press, 1973)
8 Cooke, Ivan, *op. cit.*
9 White Eagle, *Morning Light on the Spiritual Path* (White Eagle Publishing Trust, 1975)

Further Reading

Beard, Paul, *Living On* (Allen & Unwin, 1980)

Brown, Rosemary, *Unfinished Symphonies* (Pan, 1971)

Butler, Patrick, *The Healing Hand Book* (Quantum, 1990)

Conan Doyle, Sir Arthur, *History of Spiritualism* (Psychic Press, 1989)

Crossley, Alan, *The Story of Helen Duncan* (Arthur H. Stockwell Ltd 1975)

—, *The Enigma of Psychic Phenomena* (privately published, 1974)

Edwards, Harry, *A Guide to Spirit Healing* (Psychic Press, 1991)

Hall, Judy, *The Karmic Journey* (Arkana, 1990)

Harrison, Tom, *Visits by our Friends From the Other Side* (privately published, 1989)*

Inglis, Brian, *Natural and Supernatural* (Hodder & Stoughton, 1977)

—, *Science and Parascience* (Granada, 1985)

Manning, Matthew, *The Strangers* (W.H. Allen, 1978)

Moody, Raymond, *Life After Life* (Bantam, 1975)

O'Brien, Stephen, *Visions of Another World* (Aquarian Press, 1989)

—, *Voices From Heaven* (Aquarian Press, 1991)

—, *In Touch With Eternity* (Bantam Books, 1992)

Permitt, Cyril, *Photographing the Spirit World* (Aquarian Press, 1983)

Playfair, Guy Lyon, *This House is Haunted* (Sphere, 1980)

Polge, Coral, *Living Images* (Aquarian Press, 1991)

Rogo, D. Scott, *Life After Death* (Aquarian Press, 1986)

—, *The Infinite Boundary* (Aquarian Press, 1988)

Wilson, Colin, *Afterlife* (Grafton, 1985)

* Copies can be obtained from T.W. Harrison, 27 Wood Lane Close, Flackwell Heath, High Wycombe, Bucks. HP10 9EP

Useful Addresses

Allan Kardec Study Group
105 Church Hill
Walthamstow
London E17 3BD

ASSAP (The Association for the Scientific Study of Anomalous
Phenomena)
20 Paul Street
Frome
Somerset BA11 1DX

Atlantis Bookshop
49a Museum Street
London WC1A 1LY

College of Psychic Studies
16 Queensberry Place
London SW7 2EB

Confederation of Healing Organisations
113 Hampstead Way
London NW11 7JN

Greater World Christian Spiritualist Association
3/5 Conway Street
London W1P 5HP

Guild of Spiritualist Healers
3 Mayberry Gardens
Hawthorn Lea
Sandyhills
Glasgow G32 OEW

Inlight House
Waggoners Wells Lane
Grayshott
Hindhead
Surrey GU26 6DT

Institute of Spiritualist Mediums
20 Oakhurst Avenue
East Barnet
Hertfordshire EN4 8DL

National Federation of Spiritual Healers
Old Manor Farm Studio
Church Street
Sunbury-on-Thames
Middlesex TW16 6RG

Noah's Ark Society for Physical Mediumship
Tree Tops
Hall Road
Cromer
Norfolk NR27 9JQ

Psychic News
2 Tavistock Chambers
Bloomsbury Way
London WC1A 2SE

Society for Psychical Research
49 Marloes Road
London W8 6LA

Spiritualist Association of Great Britain
33 Belgrave Square
London SW1 8QL

Survival Joint Research Committee Trust
47 Mayfield Road
Hornsey
London N8 9LL

White Eagle Lodge
New Lands
Brewells Lane
Liss
Hampshire GU33 7HY
and
9 St Mary Abbots Place
London W8 6LS

Wimbledon Spiritualist Church
136 Hartfield Road
London SW19 3TJ